The First Merry Widow

Leann Richards

The First Merry Widow
The Life of Carrie Moore

The First Merry Widow: The Life of Carrie Moore
ISBN 978 1 74027 620 5
Copyright © Leann Richards 2010

First published 2010
Reprinted 2018

Ginninderra Press
PO Box 3461 Port Adelaide 5015
www.ginninderrapress.com.au

Contents

Early years	7
Djin Djin and Matsa	11
From Child Star to Diva	16
The Royal Comic Opera Company	20
Florodora and the Tyson Affair	24
Sharing the Stage	29
Carrie Departs	31
Musical Comedy in England	34
The Merry Widow and the Bigwood Scandal	40
Return to England	48
Australasian Vaudeville Star	52
Her Own Company	56
Aladdin	60
The Early War Years	65
Remarriage and the Later War Years	70
Legend	74
The Final Curtain	81
Notes	86

Early years

In 1882 Geelong, in the colony of Victoria, was a bustling seaside port with many industries and businesses. July was cold that year, and the town's prosperity did not reach to the waterfront area of Foundry Lane. Mary Moore, twenty-seven and heavily pregnant, was having a difficult time; her husband Robert was a labourer but never seemed to earn enough to support his growing family.

On Monday 31 July 1882, Mary gave birth to her third child. It was a girl. Mary and Robert named her Caroline Ellen.

Carrie was a bubbly child with a big personality and curly dark hair. The family called her 'the little exhibitionist'. She inherited her mother's love of singing, and as a child learned all the popular songs of the day. Her favourite was 'The Man Who Broke the Bank at Monte Carlo'.

By the time she was twelve, Carrie was singing gaily to her friends and neighbours who were impressed by her talent and said she should go on stage.

Mary Moore had a brother, William Wyatt, who lived in Albury. It was a beautiful area of grazing land and dairy farming and Robert and Mary would take their family there for visits. On one occasion, Carrie asked Uncle William if she and her cousin Alice could sing at a local amateur concert. Uncle William agreed, and Carrie made her stage debut.

> I came out in costume and didn't I just fancy myself. I got an encore too and later in the evening I did a sketch with my cousin Miss Alice Wyatt. It was a comic domestic squabble and I was the husband. It took immensely and I was a proud girl, I can tell you.

Carrie Moore was stage-struck.

When the family returned to Geelong, Carrie was keen to continue her stage career and her next appearance was singing at a benefit for the family of a boy who had been killed at the Geelong railway station. The girl was making an impression as a singer and stage performer in amateur circles in Geelong. Although she was young, Uncle William thought she had the potential to be a star. He had a home in Melbourne and was a member of the exclusive Melbourne Club. As such, he had the opportunity to meet several people in the theatrical community. William invited Carrie to visit and one night he asked members of the famous London Gaiety Company to his home so they could meet his talented relative.

The company was touring in 1895 and consisted of the world's best musical performers. Based at the Gaiety Theatre in London, it was famous for its high-class productions of modern musical comedies. The company that came to Australia starred Grace Palotta, a very talented performer who was a great favourite with Australian audiences.

Whilst this illustrious company was at William's home, he persuaded his young niece to sing her old favourite, 'The Man who Broke the Bank'. Grace Palotta was so impressed with the girl's performance that she offered to take her back to London. However, Mary Moore refused to allow it.

> I longed to go, but I knew that my mother would never hear of it, and it nearly broke my heart for two or three days.

Despite her love of singing, Mary was not keen on her daughter pursuing a theatrical career.

What happened next became part of Carrie's legend. Through the influence of Uncle William, she met the man who would launch her career. His name was J.C. Williamson.

In 1895, fifty-year-old James Cassius (J.C.) Williamson was the most famous person in Australian legitimate theatre. Williamson managed an empire of theatres around the country, including the prestigious Princess in Melbourne and the Royal in Sydney. He was also responsible for the Gaiety Company's successful tour of Australia. Williamson was an

American who came to Australia with his wife Maggie Moore in 1874. It was their first tour and in their repertoire was a play called *Struck Oil*, which had been a great success in the United States. Five years later, they returned to Australia and presented the first authorised production of *HMS Pinafore* in the country. Williamson had exclusive rights to the piece and vigorously upheld them, asking repeatedly for court orders to stop infringement. Gilbert and Sullivan were so impressed with his zeal in this matter that they granted him exclusive rights to their musicals in Australia. On this basis, the Williamson theatrical empire was founded.

In 1891 after almost twenty years of marriage, Maggie left J.C. for a younger man. Williamson was furious and by 1895 was cynical and bitter about the fairer sex. The depression of the 1890s had hit him hard, but he had hung on to his monopoly in legitimate theatre by a series of adroit business manoeuvres and mergers with other managers. By 1895 he was in desperate financial straits and hoped to revive his fortunes by producing a pantomime he had co-written, called *Djin Djin*.

Williamson was also a member of the exclusive gentleman's club, The Melbourne Club. He was accustomed to fellow members boasting about the theatrical talents of their relatives, so it was not a surprise when William Wyatt approached him about his niece, Carrie Moore. Williamson agreed to meet the thirteen-year-old girl, and Uncle William took Carrie on a trip to the theatre. In order to save her from nervousness, William did not tell her where they were going. He merely asked her to accompany him and sing for some friends.

Carrie recalled,

> I was willing enough and we came to town, and walked up Spring Street. As he stopped at the Princess Theatre, I saw the words 'Stage Door' written up and said, 'But this is a theatre, Uncle. What are we doing here?'

Her uncle indicated that they should go in, but Carrie was shocked. This was not a place that a proper young lady should go. However, her uncle soon persuaded her to walk through the open door.

> [I] followed him upstairs to the crush room, with my heart bumping

in my ears; There were several gentlemen there, and I was told to sing to them.

Carrie sang 'Lizzie's Farewell' from *Struck Oil*, a song that had been made famous by Maggie Moore, the former Mrs Williamson. After singing, Carrie, who had heard the noise of rehearsals, ran off and peeked through the doors at the actors. She was more interested in seeing the rehearsals than she was in singing for the strange men.

The gentlemen, one of whom was J.C. Williamson, were impressed by her sweet soprano voice. Williamson was moved to tears by her rendition of his former wife's song. Carrie was called back and one of the men, she did not know who it was, placed a hand on her arm, and looked seriously into her deep brown eyes.

'Would you like to go on the stage, little girl?' asked J.C. Williamson.

'Rather,' Carrie replied enthusiastically, and with that one little word, thirteen-year-old Carrie Moore's life was changed forever.

Djin Djin and Matsa

The 1890s were a period of depression in Australia due to a dramatic fall in the price of wool, combined with years of land speculation. Unemployment was high and several investors lost their life savings in bank collapses.

J.C. Williamson was having a difficult time too. Theatre was a luxury and one of the first activities hit by economic hard times. In addition, Williamson was having trouble booking overseas stars because theatre in Britain and the United States was booming. No international star wanted the long trip to Australia when employment was so plentiful at home.

So Williamson had to improvise. Together with Bert Royle, he decided to write and stage a lavish original pantomime. Pantomime was very popular in Australia and Williamson hoped that a combination of Australian nationalism and exotic orientalism would attract huge audiences. He and Royle wrote a Japanese fairy tale called *Djin Djin*. J.C. had invested heavily in the show and it starred his most prestigious performers, including diva Florence Young, comedian William Elton, and a group of talented children.

Williamson was very fond of children and one of Carrie's earliest memories was of the boss buying milk and buns for them during rehearsals. When they performed, the youngsters had female chaperones who dressed and undressed them and ensured their safe return home.

At Carrie's fateful meeting with J.C., he had asked her to start work immediately in *Djin Djin*. The thirteen-year-old arrived an hour early on the first Monday. She was eager and excited to learn that she would be playing the part of Prince Omni, the shogun's son who was transformed into a baboon. However, the excitement soon turned to trepidation when she attended the dress rehearsal.

> The dress I was to wear was just like that of Nanki Poo in the *Mikado*, a kind of short coat and tights. Now at the first dress rehearsal…[I] thought that the little coat reaching just down to my waist was not finished. At that time I used to wear a red cloak, a Red Riding Hood cloak, so I got that, wrapped it around my legs and went onto the stage. Suddenly somebody shouted out, 'Make that child take that cloak off.' Of course I thought my costume would cover my legs… Finally, however, a long cloak was made for me, because they could not get me to go out in this attenuated garment."

Carrie's modesty was typical for a well brought-up young woman because showing legs in public was considered vulgar, although it was an expected part of pantomime tradition. Even at thirteen, Carrie was showing an unexpected independent spirit and it must have taken immense bravery to question the costume.

On the night of the last rehearsal, J.C. Williamson gathered the cast and explained that the company was on the verge of bankruptcy. He asked them to take a pay cut and they agreed.

Djin Djin opened to a full house at the Princess Theatre in Melbourne in December 1895. The sets were wonderful and included a realistic earthquake. The ballets were beautiful and the musical numbers ranged from opera to variety and were overwhelmingly endorsed by an enthusiastic audience. The pantomime was rapturously received by critics, every performance was packed and the Melbourne papers were laudatory.

Carrie was involved in an overwhelmingly successful production, but her part as Omni was small. Most of the time, the role was played by a man in an ape costume and it was not until the final stages of the pantomime that Carrie had a chance to shine.

However, she had an opportunity to perform in the specialty part of the show when she and fellow child star, Ivy Scott, sang a duet, the delightful song 'I Don't Want to Play in your Yard'. Ivy and Carrie had a hit with this charming ditty. The girls were ideal Victorian children, beautiful, innocent and alluring.

Djin Djin played every night in Melbourne, and had matinees on Wednesdays and Saturdays. Carrie was thirteen years old and still obliged to go to school. During the run of the pantomime she spent a great deal of time running down Collins Street, Melbourne, with a satchel of schoolbooks in her hand, rushing to rehearsals.

Djin Djin continued to attract huge houses and on its final night in February 1896 there was standing room only. Williamson had his hit show and his financial situation was rapidly improving. However, the Princess Theatre was leased to another production and *Djin Djin* had to close. The show was taken to Sydney and Carrie went with it.

Sydney was the biggest city in Australia in 1896 and it had many theatres. Vaudeville was dominated by Harry Rickards and the Tivoli, whilst the legitimate theatre was monopolised by J.C. Williamson.

Djin Djin was eagerly anticipated in the city; stories of the show's opulent staging and spectacular music had reached Sydney and the Australian characters were one of the production's attractions. It was one of the first pantomimes to feature a principal boy that was unashamedly Australian. This was Williamson's nod to the tide of nationalistic fervor sweeping the colony as Federation was being discussed.

The show opened to a huge house in April 1896 at the Lyceum theatre. All of the major players were praised by the Sydney press and two of the minor ones also received favourable mention.

The *Referee* said that

> A specialty duet 'I won't play in your back yard' right towards the end between the Misses Ivy Scott and Carrie Moore also deserves more than passing recognition. These little ladies knocked endways the work of the average serio comic.

Djin Djin played in Sydney continuously through to 15 May 1896 and was a popular and critical hit. After it finished, Carrie returned to Melbourne and went to school.

Eventually July came and Carrie turned fourteen. Her break from the stage was brief; by November she was back on stage in a revival of *Djin Djin*. The pantomime reopened at the Princess Theatre in Melbourne in November 1896 and Carrie was given a larger part as Cheekee, the Daimo's younger daughter. It played for a short season, but was merely an appetiser for a much bigger show, the 1897 pantomime spectacular. The production was called *Matsa*, and was an obvious attempt to recreate the success of *Djin Djin*. It was another original pantomime written by J.C. Williamson and Bert Royle, and combined nationalist sentiment with an exotic theme, Egypt.

Matsa starred the elite performers of the Royal Comic Opera Company. Florence Young played the principal boy, George Lauri provided the comic element, and May Pollard played the villain, the evil queen Matsa. In this show Carrie played Nokatch, a Cairo donkey boy.

> My next appearance was in *Matsa*, in which I played a Cairo donkey boy and also contributed to the speciality scene. My partner was again Ivy Scott and we worked together in coster and coon songs.

Carrie also had a solo number, 'Only Me', which was a typical Victorian song about a child pining for her mother's love. Once again, Carrie was typecast as a young child and her roles represented childhood as a time of innocence and sentimentality.

Carrie did not make a great impression in the show but this was not surprising. Newspaper reviews focused on the special effects and backgrounds and even experienced performers such as George Lauri and Florence Young were virtually ignored by critics, because their surroundings were so overwhelmingly extravagant.

The show moved to Sydney in February 1897 and critics praised the sets, backgrounds, effects and costumes but were not impressed with the plot. Despite the reservations, *Matsa* was very popular. It remained in Sydney until April, when a benefit performance was given for Florence Young, who was leaving for England.

When *Matsa* finished, Carrie was approaching her fifteenth birthday and her second year with J.C. Williamson. She had played two minor roles in two major productions and had grown accustomed to performing in front of large audiences. By the time *Matsa* was produced she had outgrown her dislike for performing in tights. Carrie had also had a minor personal success with 'I Don't Want to Play in your Yard' and had gained experience in singing duets and novelty songs. In the two pantomimes, she had been surrounded by the premier musical comedy stars of the Australian theatre. Carrie's contact with these seasoned professionals increased her own skills.

At fourteen years old, she had spent almost two years in an environment designed to produce a versatile stage performer. These early lessons were to stay with her throughout her career and helped her become a star of the legitimate and vaudeville stage.

From Child Star to Diva

After appearing in *Matsa*, Carrie's career took a new course. She was too old to play the innocent child but too inexperienced to play major roles. She was under no obligation to attend school, so she was free to travel wherever J.C. Williamson sent her. It was time for Carrie to extend her repertoire and show that she could graduate from cute child singer to adult performer.

Shortly after *Matsa* finished, Carrie had an opportunity to show her diversity. In May 1897, she joined a company led by English comedian Ernest Shand. Her first play with the company was *A Night Out*, which opened in Melbourne at the Princess Theatre in May 1897; she continued in this production until July in Sydney.

Her next show was *The Gay Parisienne* with the Royal Comic Opera Company. Her inclusion in a production by this company was recognition of her talent. It was J.C. Williamson's most popular troupe and included the elite performers of the Australian legitimate stage. They were a versatile group who could dance, sing and perform burlesque, comedy, pantomime or musical theatre. For many years Williamson relied on them to support overseas performers or to present the latest musical comedies from England.

The Gay Parisienne opened at Her Majesty's Theatre in Sydney in August 1897. Ada Willoughby, a young English actress, starred. Ada had limited experience, but the fact that she was English meant she was favoured for the leading role over aspiring Australian actresses. The Comic Opera Company was struggling to find a diva to replace Florence Young and Williamson had decided to import a star for the production. *The Gay Parisienne* was quickly followed in September by *The French Maid*, another musical comedy, and Ada starred as Suzette. However, in October she fell ill.

Carrie Moore was an ambitious and enthusiastic teenager and was eager to further her career. According to Carrie, 'I knew every part in the piece, and all the other pieces I was in.' Her youthful enthusiasm convinced the mangers to let her replace Ada, and it became her first starring role. Carrie made the most of the opportunity and did not disappoint the managers or the public.

> The one night stand led to a promotion. I got through so well that I was…regular understudy afterwards.

It was a significant leap for a young girl to make. Ada Willoughby's swift return to the production after one night may have been a reaction to the warm reviews that the young Australian received.

In November 1897, the company went to Melbourne for a short season of *The Gay Parisienne*. Alice Leamar replaced Ada Willoughby as star and was panned by critics but loved by audiences.

By December they had returned to Sydney for rehearsals of the Christmas pantomime, *Babes in the Wood*. The star of the pantomime was the temperamental and talented English actress, Ada Reeve. It was Ada's first trip to Australia and she was a lively twenty-three-year-old who started working in pantomime at age four. She appeared as the principal boy, Robin Hood, in her first Australian production.

Babes in the Wood closed in February 1898 and was followed by a short revival of *The French Maid*. Ada Reeve replaced Ada Willoughby as Suzette and opening night in Sydney was witnessed by the English cricket team. In March the company travelled to Melbourne, intending to open in *The French Maid* at the Princess Theatre on 5 March, but disaster struck.

Ada Reeve was young, rich and adventurous, and on the eve of her Melbourne debut she sprained an ankle. It was a disaster for J.C. Williamson that his expensive imported leading lady was unable to open in one of the headlining musical comedies of the year. Williamson in desperation turned to Ada's young understudy, teenager Carrie Moore.

Carrie put up her hair and stepped into the shoes of one of England's most famous actresses. It was a big break, and she was an astounding success. Carrie patterned her performance on Ada's. In fact, she was so young and inexperienced that her performance was more imitation than acting. She was only fifteen years old with two years; experience on the stage, and it was a smart decision. Ada Reeve represented the best of English theatre, and the imitation ensured that Carrie was successful in the role. Despite aping her principal, some of Carrie's own characteristics shone through. She sang and danced with a vitality and enthusiasm that typified a teenager. Her exuberance and youth charmed the critics and the audience.

J.C. Williamson was so impressed with Carrie's performance that he took her home in a cab that night. When they reached the parental home, Carrie's mother opened the door and Williamson said to her, 'I'll make a star of her, Mrs Moore.'

Carrie appeared as Suzette for several nights, her name was featured in newspaper advertisements and audiences flocked to see her. She was so believable in the adult role that few could believe that she was fifteen. One night when her mother was in the audience, she overheard a woman say, 'They claim she is only fifteen. She's twenty if she's a day.' The proud Mary Moore turned to the woman and said, 'Excuse me, she is fifteen. I should know, I was in the room when she was born.'

On 10 March Ada Reeve returned to the stage and Carrie returned to being an understudy. She had proven her ability to carry a major production and had been noticed by the man in charge, J.C. Williamson.

After several weeks, the company presented *The Gay Parisienne* and Carrie played the supporting role of Ruth. She gained good notices, which made it clear that her fame was increasing.

In May 1898 the company travelled to Adelaide in South Australia, where Ada Reeve was to open in *The French Maid*, but her bad luck with the play struck again. Ada was young and modern and like many young modern women of 1898 she was infatuated with the new bicycling craze. Unfortunately, ladies' fashions had not kept up with the fad and the usual ladies' cycling garment was a long skirt of voluminous layers. This costume was impractical for cycling and the skirts would interfere with smooth running of the wheels. Ada was probably a victim of fashion when she had a cycling accident which prevented her from appearing on the opening night in Adelaide.

Once again, Carrie stepped into the role of Suzette. By this time she was comfortable with the character and was very successful. Carrie had proved her worth as a musical comedy star. However, she was only fifteen and she had all the characteristics of a teenage girl, including an adventurous spirit. In Adelaide she was free of her mother and of Mr Williamson, so it was natural that she wanted to have some fun.

Carrie enjoyed fast driving and it was an activity which she indulged throughout her life, first with carriages and later with cars. Whilst Ada was nursing her injuries, Carrie went on a horse and buggy ride and was thrown out of the trap. She broke her collarbone. The doctor advised against performing, but Carrie was stubborn and reckless and told him, 'I won't think about it. I'll just go on.' Go on she did. She performed for three nights with her shoulder strapped to her side.

It was the end of May 1898 and in one year Carrie had played in several major productions. She had starred on opening nights in Adelaide and Melbourne and was fast becoming a prominent member of the Williamson Company.

Carrie's emergence as a leading lady was well timed. Florence Young, the company's diva, was still in England; her sister Millie who was being groomed for the role, retired from the stage in 1898; and Mary Weir, the prima ballerina of the company, also retired after marrying J.C. Williamson the same year. There was a distinct lack of female stars and the company was looking for replacements. Carrie with her clear soprano voice, her youth, charisma and vivacity was an ideal candidate. She was young and malleable, and was able to carry a star vehicle. But J.C. Williamson was a cautious man. Carrie was to spend the next year performing in minor parts and regional companies. It was not until 1899 that she became a starring member of the Royal Comic Opera Company.

The Royal Comic Opera Company

In October 1899, the Boer War began and in early November, Australian troops, still organised in colonial regiments, sailed for South Africa. The war was an opportunity for the emerging colonies to show themselves worthy of Federation.

The theatre reflected the times, patriotic themes dominated and benefits were given for causes as diverse as the patriotic fund and later for the returning wounded.

The Royal Comic Opera Company was J.C. Williamson's premier company. They were the most talented theatre performers in Australia, and in 1899 Carrie joined this elite.

The life of a member of the company was tough and required a robust constitution and a great deal of stamina. In addition to long rehearsals of taxing productions, there was extensive travel around Australia. The schedule produced talented, versatile performers but it also created highly strung, nervous men and women who lived at a pace very few could maintain. This was the life that seventeen-year-old Carrie Moore was to live unceasingly for the next four years.

When Carrie became a permanent member of the Royal Comic Opera Company in late 1899, she became a fashion model, a source of gossip and a symbol of Australian nationalism.

In November of that year, she played Maid Marian in the Royal Comic Opera production of *Robin Hood*. It was one of her favourite roles. Carrie's performance as Maid Marian gained good, but not great, notices.

> Miss Carrie Moore as Maid Marian looked pretty and acted brightly. to her fell a good deal of the singing and she acceptably utilised the small vocal means at her disposal.

Carrie's voice was limited, but her on-stage charisma overshadowed this defect.

During the run of *Robin Hood* the cast participated in a benefit for the Patriotic Fund that raised £177.

Whilst playing in *Robin Hood*, Carrie and the other members of the company were rehearsing the next pantomime, *Little Red Riding Hood*. This was the most stressful part of the company's routine. Whilst performing one production they would rehearse the next, the combination was too hectic for many and caused much anxiety amongst the cast. Fortunately, Carrie was a quick study and learnt new pieces easily.

The pantomime opened on 26 December 1899 at Her Majesty's Theatre in Sydney and was big on spectacle, short on humour and filled with patriotism. Carrie played the principal boy, Little Boy Blue. She wore several tight-fitting costumes which included boy's clothes 'of blue brocade embroidered with spangles and pearl and a form hugging uniform of the New South Wales Lancers'. In the latter outfit she led contingents of troops on stage as the orchestra played 'Soldiers of the Queen'. This was one of the most popular parts of the show.

Carrie sang several songs as principal boy, but critics expressed reservations about her voice. She started having voice lessons, but the pressures and travel requirements of the Royal Comic Opera Company limited her time. She only had a couple of lessons before the demands of work curtailed them.

Little Red Riding Hood drew good houses and made a record profit for Williamson. In January 1900 the cast performed a farewell benefit for the second contingent. Williamson, who could afford to be generous, donated the proceeds to the war effort.

At the end of February 1900, the production closed and the company prepared for the road trip to Melbourne where they opened at the Princess Theatre on 24 February. The Princess had been closed for two months, so its reopening was greeted with enthusiasm. A huge audience of all classes rolled up to the doors of the Spring Street theatre that night to see *Little Red Riding Hood*. According to *The Age* newspaper, many would have preferred more substantial fare, but the magnificence of the pantomime quelled all doubt.

Carrie's notices were better than they were in Sydney and this may have been due to her Melbourne background. The critics recognised the limitations of her voice but said 'she has learned to sing with a delicacy of expression' that made up for her shortcomings. They also noted that 'her movements are a model of ease and freedom'. It was the first mention of her graceful presence on stage, the result of early ballet lessons, and this trait was soon to become a trademark of every Carrie Moore performance.

By June, Carrie was firmly established as a major star in the Royal Comic Opera Company. She was being sought for press interviews and played the role of diva well. To one reporter she acknowledged rumours that she was working too hard – 'People say I want a rest and that the strains of constant work is killing me' – and lived up to her nickname of the 'the little exhibitionist' by extending a plump white arm to the interviewer: 'Does that look like as if I was an invalid?'

She was seventeen and resented her public image as 'Little Carrie Moore'.

> They've (the public) treated me very well, but they will not notice that I'm growing…people will continue to look on me as a youngster still and call me little Carrie Moore.

Carrie was asserting her independence and did things that were daring for a young girl. One of these was wearing make-up, which was considered vulgar by mainstream society. Leipsic, the *Sydney Mail* critic, thought she was spoilt and overindulged and he was scathing about her stage appearance in HMS *Pinafore* in Sydney that June:

> I wonder though, why many actresses think it necessary to paint their eyelids to such an extent that the eyes and brows appear an indistinguishable black mess.

In July 1900, Carrie turned eighteen and on 21 July the company premiered a new opera, *The Rose of Persia*. The production starred George Lauri and Charles Kenningham. Carrie was praised for her performance, but her make-up was criticised. Leipsic bluntly said she was 'crudely made up'.

The long season in Sydney ended in October but the Royal Comic Opera Company's schedule was never ending. That month they travelled to Brisbane, where they performed a short season of Gilbert and Sullivan at the Opera House. After that it was time to board a train and travel again but this time they bypassed Sydney and headed straight to Melbourne.

Florodora and the Tyson Affair

The Royal Comic Opera Company presented *The Rose of Persia* at the new Her Majesty's Theatre in Melbourne. It had been extensively remodelled and an entire floor had been built to provide space for an elegant crush room. The renovations were still being finished when the production opened on 29 October 1900. It was to the smell of drying paint that the Royal Comic Opera Company opened their season. Carrie played Heart's Desire and Melbourne critics said that she sang with 'great freshness and expression'.

The next month the company presented *The Old Guard*. Carrie played Murielle and *The Age* described her 'climbing the ladder which leads to success not step by step but four or five rungs at a stride'. Carrie was so popular in this production that the show had to stop repeatedly to allow her to respond to audience calls for an encore.

These performances were merely a prelude for the planned Christmas extravaganza. For the first time in her years with Williamson, Carrie was not involved in a Christmas pantomime. This was a welcome and important break.

The Christmas show was *Florodora*, a new musical that was playing successfully in London. The cast that Williamson assembled for the Australian production was the best available. Carrie played Dolores, the heroine of the piece and George Lauri, the dependable company comedian, played Tweedlepunch, a wandering phrenologist. *Florodora* was a musical comedy rather than a comic opera and the show included several variety scenes, including a 'piece of absurd fooling' between Carrie and George. In this they combined to produce a burlesque of the French acrobatic troupe, The Dartos.

Carrie and George had been acquainted since *Djin Djin*, and now they formed a comic partnership on stage that became a feature of Royal Comic Opera productions.

The combination of new musical, new theatre and elite performers ensured *Florodora*'s popularity in Melbourne. It ran through Christmas and into the new year of 1901 without a break.

In January, Queen Victoria died and her son, Edward, inherited the throne after an agonisingly long wait. The Edwardian era dawned. It was a time when many of the old Victorian values were challenged. Carrie was a part of this new generation; she was eighteen years old, a star, and the object of many admiring glances.

Actresses were like the movie stars of today. Their faces adorned newspapers, their names appeared in social pages and their postcards were sold by the thousands. They were the pinnacle of style and beauty, and had many male admirers. Carrie as the star of the biggest show over the Christmas period was the recipient of much male attention and she often received gifts and flowers after the show. She had many after-theatre invitations and temptations.

In Melbourne, Carrie was surrounded by her family. They kept her feet on the ground and her virtue in tact. In addition, her boss, J.C. Williamson, was a strict disciplinarian and kept a sharp eye on his expensive properties, including his actresses. He had always taken a personal interest in Carrie and monitored her behaviour closely. Despite the changing times, Victorian morality still held sway through most of society.

The last night of *Florodora* in Melbourne was 2 April. It had broken all Australian box office records. After the show the cast packed up and hopped on a train to Sydney, *Florodora* was to open at Her Majesty's in four days. Expectations were high and news of the production's Melbourne success had intrigued Sydney theatregoers. In order to control the expected rush, an extra booking fee was charged on first night tickets. Despite this, the theatre was full on opening night.

Florodora opened on 6 April. It was described as having a bit of everything, 'A lump of pantomime, a touch of tragedy, a hundredweight of low comedy.' In spite of its unquestioned popularity in Melbourne, the first night in Sydney had a 'cordial but not remarkable' reception.

Carrie's charm and fame drew more admirers in Sydney and in early June she received a basket of flowers from an old friend, Ernest Tyson.

Twenty-eight-year-old Ernest was a member of the millionaire Tyson clan, a family of squatters who owned vast tracts of land. Ernest's family, including mother Susan, lived in Hay in New South Wales. In early June 1901, Ernest returned from a trip to China and Japan and settled into a suite at the Hotel Australia, the haunt of upper-class visitors to Sydney. One of his first stops was Her Majesty's Theatre, where he saw Carrie in *Florodora*. The pair had met two years earlier and Ernest was one of Carrie's early suitors. However, due to her youth, their relationship had remained platonic until Ernest returned from his Asian trip. Soon the friendly relationship developed into a far more serious love affair.

Ernest fell in love with Carrie, and she, free from the restrictions of her boss and family, returned the sentiment. Carrie was excited, flattered, and head over heels in love with the handsome man from the millionaire family. Their flirtation continued through June and Ernest's after-show gifts became more intimate. On 13 June he was seen leaving the Hotel Australia and visiting a prominent Sydney jeweller. The next evening, Carrie took to the stage wearing some unusual accessories, a diamond star and a diamond swallow. She made a glittering Dolores that night. The diamonds sparkled in the stage lights for all to see, and Carrie, deeply in love, sparkled as brightly.

After the show, she announced to the cast that she and Ernest were engaged and they all toasted the happiness of the young couple with champagne. Ernest wanted to get married quickly and the date was set for 27 June. He travelled to Hay to tell his mother the good news, and to ask for some material support for his married life.

Meanwhile, Carrie organised the wedding. She made an announcement to the Sydney press and reassured fans that she would not be leaving the stage. Carrie ordered dresses from Farmers, the famed Sydney department store, and asked Mrs Jones, the florist who provided flowers for the theatre, to organise blossoms for the ceremony. In order to prevent overcrowding Carrie decided to issue tickets for the event. St James Church in Sydney was picked as the location, but no arrangements were made at the church, which was a strange oversight.

Soon there were other signs that all was not going well. The wedding date arrived, but the bridegroom did not. Carrie told friends that the wedding had been postponed, but the orders for flowers and dresses were quietly dropped.

Mrs Tyson, Ernest's mother, had not approved of the match because Carrie was an actress, an occupation that was frowned upon by some in upper-class society. Ernest had no independent fortune and, faced with disinheritance, would not stand against his mother. The family sent him to Queensland to cure him of his infatuation.

Meanwhile, Carrie remained in Sydney, working. She was rehearsing the next Royal Comic Opera Company production, *The Casino Girl*, whilst still performing in *Florodora*. On the closing night she was as vivacious as ever. She wore the diamond star and swallow on stage despite the uncertainty.

J.C. Williamson returned to Australia that August and was furious at Carrie's entanglement. That month, the Royal Comic Opera Company travelled to Brisbane and Carrie finally gave up all hope of Ernest. She lodged a breach of promise suit against him. She was suing for damages for her broken heart and probably hoping for some relief for her embarrassment. Carrie priced both at £5,000. J.C. Williamson may have encouraged her to sue, as it was unlikely that she would have pursued the case without his permission. The papers were lodged in Sydney and a date was set for December, when Carrie would be available to testify.

Whilst the wheels of justice moved slowly, Carrie had to maintain the frenetic pace of the Royal Comic Opera Company. After a brief season in Brisbane, the Company travelled to Adelaide, where they performed *Florodora*.

In early December they returned to Sydney and their leading lady had a special reason to do so. Her breach of promise suit was to be settled on 4 December.

Ernest's mother, Susan Tyson, was determined not to pay £5,000 to Carrie Moore and had hired the Attorney General of NSW to represent Ernest. Carrie had her own representative. The two gentlemen had several discussions before the court date and advised the judge on 4 December that a settlement had been reached. The details were not revealed in court, but both gentlemen informed the judge that it was an 'honourable' outcome.

Nineteen-year-old Carrie was less discreet than the honourable counsels. The Tuesday following the settlement, she ordered champagne for the cast and crew of *Florodora*. After the performance they gathered together to toast her victory over the Tysons.

Carrie had been awarded much less than £5,000, but the settlement was generous. She had been awarded £100 in damages, and was permitted to keep £400-worth of diamonds Ernest had given to her. In addition, she received £114 to cover the costs of her pre-ordered bridal dresses and £240 in court costs. It was a very satisfactory result and Carrie had every reason to celebrate. It was also the beginning of her famous diamond collection.

She was now free of Ernest and the attentions of many male admirers were balm to her shattered pride. As the leading lady of the Royal Comic Opera Company, she was established as a favourite with men and women alike throughout the eastern states of Australia. She was famous, admired and praised by all, and she was only nineteen.

Sharing the Stage

In 1897, Carrie had performed at the farewell benefit for the leading lady of the Royal Comic Opera Company, Florence Young. In 1902, Florence, known as 'Flo', returned to Australia. Florence, with her well guarded soprano voice, was a very popular performer in Australia and was welcomed home warmly.

Carrie's talents were different from Flo's. She was younger and relied on comic ability, energetic renderings of songs and gracefulness on stage to appeal to an audience. The two ladies were also different physically: Florence was voluptuous and solid in stature whilst Carrie had the slight figure of a teenager.

From the time of Florence's return, it was clear that she would take the major roles which Carrie expected. In *A Runaway Girl* that May, Florence took the leading role of Winifred whilst Carrie had to be satisfied with providing the comic element. A similar situation occurred with *A Circus Girl* in July. Carrie simply did not have the vocal equipment to compete with Flo's superbly trained voice.

In August, during the run of *Robin Hood*, critics noted that Carrie's voice seemed tired and its limitations were even more evident because of the continual presence of Florence Young's booming vocals.

Carrie had never had the opportunity to train her voice. She had been on the stage continuously since she was thirteen years old and the long nights and rehearsals were beginning to take a toll. Carrie understood that her singing had limitations but there was little she could do. Work took all her time, and she was starting to resent the demands of the Royal Comic Opera Company. Soon she was describing it as 'So exhausting sometimes and seems to make such a severe draw upon one's physical strength.'

Carrie was twenty years old and had spent the last seven years in the Williamson cocoon. She was becoming bored and tired of it.

The frantic pace of the Royal Comic Opera Company continued throughout 1902 and Carrie continued to take secondary roles. In Melbourne that November Carrie played Susan, the owner of a flower shop, whilst Florence took the major role of Donna Teresa in the premiere of *The Toreador*.

At the end of 1902 the company packed and headed to Sydney for a short Christmas season. This began with Dorothy in late December. Now Carrie realised that her time with the Royal Comic Opera Company was limited. Florence Young was the undisputed leading lady and Carrie would not advance until her retirement, which would not be in the near future. The constant comparison of the two ladies voices on stage was not helping Carrie's career. A year ago she had been taking leading roles to much acclaim and now she was reduced to supporting or comedic parts.

Carrie was twenty years old and she was tired and unhappy, but she knew little else but the Williamson Company. Her life and friends revolved around it and the lifestyle was one she enjoyed. She seemed to be stuck, but her employer J.C. Williamson was a generous man, and he knew that Carrie was restless. Once again he stepped in to guide her career.

Carrie Departs

The Royal Comic Opera Company began 1903 in Sydney. After a short season of *Dorothy*, they played *Paul Jones*. On 28 January, the company performed the Mikado. Carrie played Yum Yum and tied her hair back from her face for the part. The altered hairstyle made her look younger and showed the smooth contours of her face, it was noted favourably by critics. A revival of *Robin Hood* followed, with Carrie playing Maid Marian. Leipsic again criticised her, saying that

> The clever young soubrette had had such a busy time since she came to the front with a rush from a precocious childhood that probably she cannot tear herself away from the glamour and prominence of the footlights.

Carrie had been pampered since she was thirteen years old, with admirers who praised her and maids who served her; she was spoilt and indulged and this was necessary because of her frantic lifestyle. Carrie was also daring and constantly challenged social mores. She went on buggy rides with gentlemen friends and she wore revealing costumes and make-up. The Tyson affair had been a scandal and from that time there was always a doubt about her respectability. Her continued disregard of convention merely reinforced that doubt.

The Royal Comic Opera Company's Sydney season ended in February 1903 with *The Geisha*. The company took it to Melbourne at the end of the month. In Melbourne, Carrie was accepted as a star and her reviews were much warmer in that city.

The frenetic pace of the company continued into April. That month they performed three musicals. *Ma Mie Rosette*, *Paul Jones* and *The Toreador*. Through April the company was also preparing a new production, *My Lady Molly*.

This was Carrie's last new show with the Royal Comic Opera Company in Melbourne. J.C. Williamson had decided to guide Carrie's career in another direction, and had given her an early and unusual twenty-first birthday present. It was a contract with England's most famous producer of musical comedies, George Edwardes. Carrie was pleased and excited about the contract, her career in Australia had stalled and she thought London would give her more opportunities.

> I must step out into the world to find out what I can do there, among strangers. I want to succeed. I want to see what I can do in London

At almost twenty-one years old, Carrie was small and petite with glowing brown eyes and long dark hair. She was playful, mischievous and ambitious, but she also had a keen sense of self-awareness, particularly when it came to her work.

> My voice is improving you know, and when I get to London I hope to have more time for cultivating it under a capable teacher.

On 27 May 1903, the Royal Comic Opera Company held a complimentary farewell matinee for Carrie at Her Majesty's Theatre in Melbourne. The matinee featured Carrie in several of her most memorable performances. These included 'I Don't Want to Play in Your Yard' with Ivy Scott and the famous Dartos burlesque with George Lauri. Every lady who attended the performance was given a souvenir programme. The programme contained a special message from Carrie.

> For all your kindliness to me
> Sweet memories in my heart shall dwell
> Some day, I'll wander home again.
> Till then, dear friends, I'll say farewell.

On 2 June, Carrie and the Royal Comic Opera Company left Melbourne for Western Australia. After a short season, Carrie departed for London on 27 July. She was twenty-one years old and looking forward to conquering the city. It was the great turning point in Carrie

Moore's life. She was travelling to the city where every Australian actress wanted to succeed. The competition was fierce, but she had several advantages, including a strong professional background, a signed contract with George Edwardes and her youth. It was a potent combination, but she was still an outsider, a colonial interloper in the English scene.

Musical Comedy in England

In 1903, English musical comedy was dominated by George Edwardes. The producer, who was born in 1852, was credited with inventing the genre. Edwardes's productions involved a combination of beautiful girls and catchy songs, and his main theatre was the famous Gaiety Theatre in London. His chorus girls, called the Gaiety Girls, were the height of sophistication. Edwardian theatre fused the stage and society, so that the leading actresses of the day were also the leaders of high fashion.

The stage was also a magnet for the aristocracy, especially after Edward ascended the throne. The king was famous for his infatuation with actresses. The English aristocracy followed their sovereign's lead and many a Gaiety Girl found herself a titled husband. Despite this, the theatrical profession was still regarded as vulgar by high society and the aristocratic marriages were considered mismatches.

The George Edwardes who became Carrie's manager in 1903 was a successful and demanding businessman who was friendly with royalty. He was very pedantic and oversaw every detail of his productions. Lecherous aristocrats eyed Edwardes's actresses over the footlights and the demanding manager expected perfection. Twenty-one-year-old Carrie was accustomed to admiration and success, but she was unaccustomed to the scale and wealth of English society.

Carrie's first appearances in England were in the provinces; however, by December 1903 she was performing in the capital. In that month she appeared in a revival of *The Girl from Kays*. Carrie had been a star in Australia, but in England she was one of many pretty girls under contract. Her accent and her attitudes were against her, and she felt slighted and disappointed with her London reception. Yet Carrie was stubborn and ambitious and determined to succeed.

The Girl from Kays played at the Apollo Theatre through December 1903 and in January 1904 it transferred to the Comedy Theatre. English productions had much longer seasons than their Australian counterparts and playing the same role for a period of months was a luxury for Carrie, who was accustomed to the fast pace of the Royal Comic Opera Company.

It was not until March 1904 that Carrie had her first stand-out role in an original and successful show. It was called *The Cingalee*.

George Edwardes, like J.C. Williamson, knew that productions with an Eastern or Asian setting were popular with audiences. Musicals such as *The Geisha* and *San Toy* had been very successful, and they allowed costumiers and scenarists the latitude to be extravagant. *The Cingalee* was a production that exploited the public's fascination with everything Oriental.

Carrie's physical attributes made her suitable for the role of Naitooma, a girl on a tea plantation, but her complexion was too fair for a genuine 'Cingalee'. This was not important to Edwardes; a Gaiety Girl had a certain style and image to project which included porcelain skin and an attractive figure. Carrie's role was little more than decoration.

According to Carrie, she thought the make-up was wrong for the role and in a move reminiscent of her thirteen-year-old objection to the *Djin Djin* outfit, she made her displeasure known. She confronted Edwardes and refused to wear white make-up. This was an audacious act for a little known Australian and Edwardes, the most powerful producer in England let her know it was inappropriate. 'Remember, you are not in Australia now.'

Carrie replied, 'Don't be such an old fathead. I'm supposed to be playing a Cingalee, aren't I? Have you ever seen a white Cingalee?'

According to legend, Carrie won the argument and in postcards of the production she clearly has darkened skin.

The Cingalee played in London for a year and Carrie remained with the production until the end of 1904. During the run, she had a song written for her and it was such a popular success that it held up the show. Edwardes was incensed that she was detracting from his established stars, and had the song removed. Such attention conflicted with his philosophy that the show came before the actors, but Carrie had other ideas,

'Your stars are old women. I'm much better than your so-called stars.'

George Edwardes did not take kindly to her forthright pronouncements and it was clear that Carrie was not happy with his management. She was disappointed that her career in London was not as meteoric as it had been in Australia. Carrie was looking for the fast track to fame and fortune, and she found it with another theatrical impresario, Robert Courtneidge.

After the conclusion of *The Cingalee*, Carrie was banished to the provinces. She was eager to break her contract with Edwardes but had no way of doing so.

Courtneidge suggested a strategy. 'When he [Edwardes] asks if you would like to play pantomime, you say, "Oh no, only old women play pantomime." He'll let you go.'

Carrie followed the advice, and Edwardes let her go.

Ironically, her first role for the new manager was in pantomime. She played the principal boy in the Christmas 1904 production of *Aladdin* at the Shakespeare Theatre in Liverpool.

In August 1905 Carrie played under Courtneidge's management in *The Blue Moon* at London's Lyric Theatre. The production was one of the manager's first forays as a producer- director. Carrie played Millicent Leroy, a maid, to Billie Burke's Evelyn Ormsby. The professional relationship between the two actresses soon became a lifelong friendship.

In March 1906, *The Blue Moon* closed, and in April 1906 Carrie was assigned another role which was to become her most famous London performance. That month Courtneidge presented *The Dairymaids* and it immediately became a popular and critical hit. Carrie played Peggy, a dairymaid, but it was her striking appearance as the Sandow Girl that garnered critical praise and audience approval. As the Sandow Girl, Carrie was dressed in little more than clinging material.

> In the draperies of the Sandow girl…which assume voluminous proportions about the feet but which vanish into nothingness as they approach the shoulders, she is quite a model of classic grace and her movements…are beyond praise in their lissomness and their display of beautiful feminine muscularity.

Carrie was a sensation. Her obvious physical charms were displayed prominently in the tight-fitting Sandow costume. She was mentioned in *The Theatre Magazine*, and quoted in *Photo Bits*. She made sure that the publicity portrayed her as a modern and slightly risqué girl, which added to the naughty attraction of the part. In *Photobits* she asserted that she was a keen believer in the corsetless style.

> I think we symmentrian girls should be looked upon as a sort of practical illustration of a great and natural theory that the human form can even in the twentieth century look quite pleasant and up to date without the help of a squeeze in trellis work surrounding the middle of the body and reducing it to the proportions of an eggcup.

It was a daring admission, typical of Carrie's forthright Australian style. It also agreed with the Sandow philosophy, so it maintained the image that lead to Carrie's greatest success.

Her success was due to years of playing everything from principal boy to diva with the Royal Comic Opera Company. This experience had given her grace and charisma on stage. The role also suited her personality and it drew upon her ability to challenge convention whilst remaining respectable.

The result of Carrie's fame as the Sandow Girl was an increase in requests for photographs. The Edwardian age was the time of the postcard craze, and cards of actresses were very popular. Carrie's image was reproduced on thousands of cards and she was contracted to English photographers Foulsham and Bandfield. The pictures showed Carrie in bonnets and in formal and informal situations and in most she wore corsets and a demure expression. The most popular photographs were of her in the Sandow costume. Soon Carrie was autographing over a hundred postcards a day. She usually signed with a simple and ambiguous 'Yours always, Carrie Moore.'

The Dairymaids continued until December 1906. Carrie had gained the fame she desired with Courtneidge and was happy to continue with his management.

Fame in London brought male admirers, and Carrie's daring performance as the Sandow Girl brought some welcome and unwelcome attention. One of her suitors was William Proctor. Before 1907 William was an insurance clerk earning £500 a year. However, that year he inherited a large sum from his deceased father, which gave him an independent income of £1,500 a year, effectively tripling his wealth. William became reckless with his money. He also became infatuated with London's newest sensation, Carrie Moore. In order to impress the lady, William began buying jewellery. Naturally Carrie's preference was for diamonds.

During 1907, William gave her many expensive gifts including brooches, pins, bracelets and earrings. They included a diamond ring worth £850 which William considered an engagement ring. Overall, he spent £3,052 on jewellery for the Australian diva. It was twice his yearly income and eventually led to bankruptcy. William was one of Carrie's most favoured admirers.

She had many fans. She later told of how the King and the Duke of Windsor would lean over the Royal box, leering and smiling at her on stage.

> I could have retired into British aristocracy as so many stage ladies did, but I couldn't fall in love with a title. I had plenty of opportunities.

Despite the gifts of diamonds and the flattery of important men, Carrie cherished an idea of romantic love. However, it was not a purely idealistic notion and was mixed with a strong sense of practicality. Carrie had been hurt by Ernest, and was careful with her heart.

In April 1907, Courtneidge produced an original play, *Tom Jones*.

Carrie played Honour, a waiting woman. Her performance was noted by the London *Times*, which commented that she made 'a duly arch waiting woman'.

Carrie continued to perform under Courtneidge's management and appeared in vaudeville and pantomime. In December 1907 she was in Birmingham playing in the pantomime *Cinderella*. Carrie was the principal boy and Phyllis Dare played Cinderella. During one performance, an old friend was in the audience. He came backstage and had a proposal for Carrie. It was J.C. Williamson and he wanted her to return to Australia as the star of the new sensation, *The Merry Widow*.

The Merry Widow and the Bigwood Scandal

During Carrie's absence from Australia, Williamson and the Royal Comic Opera Company had continued to present the latest offerings from London. Williamson was looking for a star who would boost the company and was anxious to present *The Merry Widow* in Australia. The musical had opened at Daly's Theatre in London in June 1907 to great acclaim. The English translation of a Viennese opera, it concerned the affairs of a rich widow, Sonia, who sought love with a former admirer Danilio. Its charm was the music by Franz Lehar and *The Merry Widow* waltz soon became a popular hit around the world.

Carrie was the ideal choice to play Sonia. Her return to Australia brought publicity for the company and her success in London brought cachet to the production. She was a local girl bringing her international fame home, a patriotic gesture that was appreciated by Australian audiences.

When Carrie returned to Australia, she came as an international musical comedy star. No longer 'little Carrie Moore', one of the divas of the Royal Comic Opera Company, she was now Carrie Moore, London actress. She expected to be treated like an international star too.

Saturday 18 May 1908 was an amazing night for Her Majesty's Theatre in Melbourne. A well dressed and eager crowd thronged the theatre to witness the premiere of the *The Merry Widow* starring Melbourne's own Carrie Moore. The theatre was buzzing with excitement and anticipation. When J.C. Williamson took his seat, there was a warm burst of applause and he politely bowed and tipped his hat to the audience. The lights lowered and the theatre hushed. Carrie made her first appearance on stage and there was a roar of recognition. It was clear that she had developed a graceful and charismatic stage presence whilst in London. Her voice was still weak, but her acting and projection skills had improved in the large theatres of the English capital.

Carrie was joined on stage by Australia's favorite diva Florence Young, who played Natalie. Florence's sweet clearly enunciated soprano had lost none of its power and quality and Carrie's voice continued to suffer by comparison. However, the fact that Carrie was taking the primary role and Florence was supporting her would have soothed any jealousy on Carrie's side.

The highlight of the show was *The Merry Widow* waltz performed by Carrie and Andrew Higginson, who played Danilio. Its music was already familiar to Melbourne audiences and the dance that accompanied it was sensational. Carrie and Andrew twirled in a Slavic-influenced romp that got faster as the music grew louder. Finally and dramatically they disappeared to the resounding cheers of the spectators. Carrie was described as being 'dreamily alluring' as she danced. It was a compliment to her ability to show poise on stage, and echoed her triumph as the Sandow Girl in London.

When the show finished, the stage was covered by flowers. The audience demanded J.C. Williamson, and the Guv'nor obliged by appearing and making a short speech. Flanked by a smiling Carrie, he stated that it was as fine a production as he had seen anywhere in the world. J.C. was justifiably proud, as the operetta had met all his expectations.

The Merry Widow played in Melbourne for eleven weeks and every night the audience packed the theatre and erupted into applause when the waltz was performed. Carrie spent her limited leisure time visiting friends and entertaining admirers. On one trip her car broke down and she was stuck in the middle of the Victorian countryside. There was a real danger that she would miss her next performance.

Carrie frantically waved down a cart driven by a local farmer. 'I'm Carrie Moore, the actress. My car's broken down. You'll take me to Melbourne, won't you? I'm in a desperate hurry to get to the theatre.'

The farmer, obviously a traditionalist with conservative values answered, 'I'll have no actress, daughter of the devil, in my cart. My horse'd drop dead. Off with you, woman.'

It was a stark reminder of the continued disapproval of actresses by certain sections of the community. Fortunately, Carrie's leading man, Andrew Higginson, passed by half an hour later. He found Carrie weeping sorrowfully on the side of the road, gently ushered her into his car and took her back to the theatre.

There were many who disapproved of the acting profession and saw actresses as fallen women. But there were many more who were anxious to bathe in the glow of the famous. Carrie had many admirers in Melbourne and she was worshipped by audiences and showered with gifts. One was a young man called Percy Bigwood, an Englishman, who sat in the front row of the theatre every night trying to catch Carrie's eye.

Although the Australian press called him Percy Plantagenet Bigwood, Percy's middle name was the less dignified Partridge. He was born in the Parish of Bromogrove, Worrcestershire, England in December 1881, which made him a few months older than Carrie. When he was nineteen he was still in Worcestershire, working as a clerk. Later that year he travelled to South Africa and remained in the Capetown area for four years. In 1905, heavily in debt, he returned to England via Ceylon and Switzerland. During the Swiss stopover he met a young girl named Ivy Salvin and the next year he and Ivy went to New Zealand. Whilst there, Percy pursued a variety of occupations including working on the literary staff of the newspaper *The Evening Post*. In 1907 he accepted an appointment to the staff of the New Zealand *Referee*. He also became manager of an amusement park, and was sued for nonpayment of rent. Percy was not very good with money. He probably used his press contacts to obtain tickets to *The Merry Widow* and soon he was making nightly visits to the production.

Percy was a tall, dark-haired, clean-shaven man, whose close-cropped locks, square chin and long straight nose gave him an air of command and directness. He bore a striking resemblance to Carrie's first fiancé, Ernest Tyson. He was a charmer, conventionally handsome, and was smooth in social situations. Carrie, who had just returned to Australia and was readjusting to Australian society, was enchanted with his good manners and gentlemanly style. Percy reportedly owned racehorses and the pair attended the races together in Melbourne. He was also a gambler who liked to place extravagant bets. He had been in financial trouble before and was in the habit of borrowing money from lady friends.

When *The Merry Widow* finished its Melbourne run, the cast and crew travelled to Sydney and Percy followed.

At midday on Saturday 26 September, a crowd gathered outside Her Majesty's Theatre in Sydney seeking tickets to *The Merry Widow*. That evening a stellar audience, which included Australian opera star Ada Crossley and J.C. Williamson, watched Carrie conquer the city.

When she first appeared on stage, the audience reaction was so loud and long that it stopped the show. The same reception was accorded all the principal performers. During the interval, an organ grinder outside the theatre entertained smokers with a version of *The Merry Widow* waltz.

It was the waltz that charmed the city. When the audience returned to the theatre, they saw Carrie and Andrew perform the dance. They went 'ratty' as the music played. Carrie's elegant stage presence captivated the crowd as Higginson twirled her around the stage to the bewitching tune.

When the show ended, J.C. Williamson, hand in hand with Carrie Moore, bowed to the audience. J.C.'s protégée had returned home and was triumphant. It was a special moment for both of them. Carrie finally had the recognition that she wanted and J.C. had the pleasure of seeing his promise to Mrs Mary Moore come true. He had 'made a star' of little Carrie Moore. It was a remarkable occasion and the audience applauded rapturously, flowers filled the stage and the cast bowed and smiled as the curtain fell. It was a hugely successful night and Carrie was the talk of Sydney.

Days later, her fame was no less, but the talk was not about her performance but about scandal. The Merry Widow had secretly eloped with Percy Bigwood.

Theatrical Sydney was disappointed in the secrecy and would have loved a big wedding. But Carrie and Percy had snuck away to a small Congregational church and married quietly in the presence of a few friends and Carrie's sister Eva. Immediately following the wedding, Percy and Carrie called on Mrs J.C. Williamson. She immediately informed her famous husband of the match.

J.C. Williamson was not impressed with his leading lady's impulsive elopement. To him, work was more important than love, and Carrie had disrupted his premier show. Carrie's marriage caused a permanent rift between her and the man who had made her career and the consequences endured for decades. The situation was exacerbated by the impetuosity of the elopement. It was so sudden that Ivy Scott, Carrie's understudy, had to rehearse all night at the Williamson home in order to replace Carrie.

Mr and Mrs Bigwood had a brief honeymoon and then settled into a home on Billyard Avenue, Elizabeth Bay, in the heart of theatrical Sydney. While Carrie took a break, her old friend, Ivy, who had once sung 'I won't play in your backyard', filled in.

It seemed that Carrie had finally found happiness with Percy. He was handsome, attentive and very fond of his new wife. However, a storm was brewing and it came with the Melbourne Express in the form of Ivy Salvin.

Ivy had shared the boat to Australia with Percy, and the two had lived in New Zealand for almost two years before Percy had begun his quest for Carrie. They had previously been acquainted in England and Ivy had often used the name Mrs Bigwood. Whilst *The Merry Widow* was playing, she had stayed near Melbourne with her two children and Percy later admitted that he was their father.

On 1 October, Ivy had received a wire, telling her of Percy's wedding and she had immediately set out for Sydney. On 3 October, she arrived via the Melbourne Express and headed straight to the office of solicitor, Mr Carroll. Ivy claimed that Percy had promised marriage, and Carroll immediately issued a writ for breach of promise.

The solicitor and Ivy, accompanied by the police, then travelled to Sydney's eastern suburbs, and the police impounded a car belonging to Percy. Ivy claimed the vehicle was bought with her money. Later that day, when Percy and Carrie were preparing to attend the races, they discovered that the car was unavailable. The newlyweds caught a cab instead.

The situation caused a sensation in Sydney. It was covered avidly in the local press. The *Sydney Morning Herald* called it a 'Theatrical Cause Célèbre' and it was lampooned in illustrations and verse.

It was generally accepted that Bigwood and Miss Salvin were married. However, Percy emphatically denied the Breach of Promise charge saying that 'There was never any promise of marriage between that lady and myself', although he admitted that he had known Ivy for two or three years in New Zealand and England.

Carrie made no public comments on the situation, merely ignoring press questions saying that she and her husband were late for a dinner engagement.

The couple hired Arthur Deery, a solicitor married to actress Aggie Thorne, to fight the legal action. Mr Deery used his wife's connections to find a suitable settlement for the parties. The situation was quickly and quietly resolved. Ivy received £1,500 pounds and also gained a role in the Meynell and Gunn production of *The Belle of Mayfair*.

She was pleased that the suit was settled. 'I shall be able to go on lightheartedly now,' she told reporters. Her pleasure was increased by the fact that she was granted the disputed car. 'I drove to the races in it this afternoon and seemed to cause a great deal of interest.'

Mr and Mrs Bigwood were also at the races that afternoon.

Ivy received proposals of marriages and she seemed to revel in her new-found celebrity.

Soon after the suit was settled, Mr Percy Bigwood visited his wife at

Her Majesty's Theatre and proceeded to Randwick Racecourse. Whilst there he placed a large bet on the horse Mooltan, which subsequently won the Metropolitan Cup. After the first act of *The Merry Widow*, Carrie received a wire from her husband saying that he had won £500, and she was elated at the result.

Audiences flocked to the show, encouraged by the opportunity to see the famous Mr Bigwood in person. On most nights he sat in the front row watching his wife perform.

After the scandal, reviewers became colder towards Carrie's performance. Her reputation obviously affected the notices. *The Sportsman* said when Ivy Scott briefly filled in, 'Miss Scott…gives an infinitely better performance than Mrs. Bigwood.'

Carrie was stubborn and she often defied convention. After the Bigwood affair, a scent of scandal surrounded her name. From this point, Australian newspaper reviews of Carrie's performances often commented on her vulgarity or lack of it. In Edwardian society, women were expected to conform to conservative social mores. The independent, headstrong Carrie was an object of scorn for many reviewers, although audiences were more forgiving. The withdrawal of J.C. Williamson's protection also allowed the press to be more vocal in their condemnation.

Carrie must have known about Ivy before she married Percy, but it seems she believed her husband's protestations that the two were not married. However, Carrie probably did not know that there was another Mrs Bigwood in England. This lady, Bessie Jackson Bigwood, had married Percy in South Africa in November 1901. They had lived together for the four years that Percy was in that country, and had one child together. In April 1905, Percy had sent Bessie and the child back to England, but when he met Ivy, he deserted them. Percy, however, had kept in contact with Bessie, especially when finances were grim. Before sailing to New Zealand he had borrowed money from her and made promises of reconciliation. However, these came to nothing, and Percy had left England with Ivy Salvin. Perhaps Ivy too was unaware of

Bessie, but this was unlikely. What is clear is that Percy had contracted a bigamous marriage with Carrie Moore, and Carrie, deeply in love, did not know it.

In November, as she and Percy sailed to England to fulfil an engagement in *Cinderella* for Robert Courtneidge, Carrie was about to experience changes in her private and public life. The next decade was to be one of fluctuating fortunes for Australia's own Carrie Moore.

Return to England

Carrie and Percy had created a scandal in Australia by their hasty marriage. Their return to London therefore fulfilled two purposes. It met Carrie's commitment to Robert Courtneidge and relieved the relentless pressure of the Australian press.

Carrie was committed to working in Courtneidge's Christmas 1908 pantomime *Cinderella*. It was a joint production with her old employer George Edwardes and had a stellar cast. The pantomime was the biggest London production that Christmas and played for several months. After its conclusion, Carrie took some time off stage to concentrate on her troubled marriage.

There were already storms on the horizon. Early in 1909, Percy had written to his first wife, Bessie Bigwood, and arranged to meet her. Bessie begged him to return to her and their child. She had heard of Percy's involvement with Carrie through the newspapers and was stunned.

Whether it was the presence of Bessie or for other reasons, Carrie decided to retire from the stage. It was a short-lived decision. Soon she was offered a role in a new London musical, *The Persian Princess*.

> I gave up the stage in England… I decided to retire but my resolution only lasted three months. Then I received an offer to appear in *The Persian Princess*.

The musical comedy opened in April 1909 at the Queens Theatre in London, and opened to awful reviews. The play had a short and disappointing run despite the presence of an experienced and well regarded cast.

In the midst of this professional disappointment, Carrie suffered more humiliation in her personal life. Percy arranged to meet the ever-persistent Bessie at his mother's grave. It was an emotional meeting. Bessie again asked Percy to give up his adulterous ways but Percy refused to admit that his marriage to Carrie was bigamous.

But Percy was not the only one with a chequered romantic history, Carrie's past was also catching up with her. In June, William Proctor appeared in bankruptcy court. All the intimate details of their liaison appeared in the papers in London and Australia.

Proctor testified that he had become engaged to Carrie in November 1907, mere months before her departure for Australia. He had spent over £3,000 on twenty-four items of jewellery and this included a single stone diamond ring valued at £850. Under questioning, Proctor stated that this was an engagement ring for Carrie Moore. The court determined that Proctor had spent thousands of pounds on jewellery for the Australian actress.

Collecting jewellery was a hobby for Carrie. Her youthful involvement with Ernest Tyson had lead to a lifelong quest for diamonds. The gentlemen who courted her were expected to indulge her passion and William Proctor had been obsessed with Carrie. The case was complicated by the fact that Carrie had admitted in interviews that she was engaged to William.

The newspapers published the scandalous details of their relationship. In Australia, they began to question the legality of Carrie's marriage to Percy.

So intense was the gossip that Percy was forced to write letters to the press. He assured the newspapers that his relationship with Carrie was legitimate, and New Zealand paper *The Otago Witness* added its own testimonial calling the rumours 'untrue and without foundation'. Mr Bigwood also told the press that he and Carrie were planning a joint vaudeville appearance.

The stresses in her personal life combined with the failure of *The Persian Princess* caused Carrie to rethink the course of her career. Carrie later cited the failed production as 'the indirect cause of my going on the vaudeville stage'.

However, her next major appearance was in pantomime. Still under contract to Courtneidge, Carrie appeared in his Christmas 1909 production of *Dick Whittington*. The show was staged at Liverpool's Shakespeare Theatre, the heart of Courtneidge's operation. It ran for several months and the financial rewards may have given Carrie the confidence to finally change the focus of her career. It was around this time that she decided to forsake musical comedy and concentrate on vaudeville or variety.

She later gave a reporter the reasons for her decision:

There are less opportunities perhaps from an artistic standpoint, but there are appreciable advantages of less work and more money. No financial risks no rehearsals, no three hour performances! Why, vaudeville is an artist's paradise after years of close study and hard practice for musical comedy and comic opera.

Carrie put these thoughts into action and by August 1910 she was appearing at the Tivoli in London as a vaudeville artist. But the decision was not final. That year she also did a tour of the provinces as the lead in *Our Miss Gibbs* under George Edwardes's management. It was an odd decision and perhaps her vaudeville performances were not sufficiently profitable. Whatever the reason, it was a significant change from the glory days of *The Dairymaids*.

There was also the continued problem of Bessie. Whilst Carrie and Percy were in Dublin that year, Bessie was also in the city. There was another confrontation with Percy. Carrie must have known of the woman's persistence and it would have caused her great distress.

In March 1911 Carrie was still touring the provinces and she played in *The Dairymaids* in Glasgow.

The next year, Carrie returned to vaudeville and the decision was final. She made several provincial appearances and performed at the Alhambra in London in a variety turn which consisted of songs and sketches.

However, the spectre of her husband's past would not rest. In January 1912, Bessie, despairing of Percy, served him with divorce papers. When Percy received the papers he signed a confession detailing his affair with Ivy Salvin and the two children who had resulted from the liaison, but he refused to admit that his marriage to Carrie was illegal.

In April 1912, the case reached the courts and the London *Times*. The article in the *Times* gave detailed information about Percy's marriage to Bessie in South Africa, his affair, his children with Ivy Salvin, and his relationship with Carrie. They were embarrassing revelations, particularly when Bessie was granted a divorce based upon her husband's 'adultery with Miss Salvin at Epsom and at Glasgow with Miss Carrie Moore and of his desertion of the petitioner'. The ruling publically branded Carrie as an adulterer and denied her the comfort of being a respectable married woman.

The marriage was in trouble but the pair resolved to stay together. By the time the case had reached the papers, Carrie and Percy were on their way to Australia. Carrie said it was to visit family, but it was also an escape from publicity.

They were soon in the southern hemisphere, and Carrie received an offer from Ben Fuller, the Australasian vaudeville entrepreneur. Fuller proposed a wage of £100 a week to return as a vaudeville performer in Australia and New Zealand. Carrie accepted and in May, Mr and Mrs P.P. Bigwood arrived in New Zealand to launch her Australasian vaudeville career.

Australasian Vaudeville Star

In April 1912, the New Zealand press announced that Fullers had signed Carrie Moore for her first appearances in that country. The papers called it 'one of the most notable engagements in the history of the firm.'

Carrie's first performance in New Zealand was at the Theatre Royal in Wellington on Monday 6 May. She was warmly greeted by a packed house. However, her turn was not entirely successful. Carrie's version of vaudeville or variety was refined and classy and it was too much so for audiences accustomed to broader and earthier fare. Her appearance was the sign of a growing trend. Many legitimate artists were appearing in the vaudeville 'halls' and managers were trying to alter their atmosphere. For many years, vaudeville had been a venue for broad humour and double entendres, but this was changing. Vaudeville owners were attempting to make their theatres and performers family friendly and less risqué. By hiring Carrie, Fullers was echoing a trend that was already apparent in England. They were using her to improve the stature of their enterprises.

Carrie remained in New Zealand for a month and then made her long awaited return to the stage in Melbourne in June 1912.

Melbourne was a city of squares, motor cars and electric trams mingling with horses, carts and hansom cabs. The latter were less common than they had once been, but the mixture of old and new was a feature of every Australian city in 1912. Life was changing. Technology was rapidly advancing and the telegraph and movie theatres were increasing their reach. The older styles of communication and entertainment were fading.

There were changes in the theatre world too. J.C. Williamson was aging and ill and Australia's king of vaudeville, Harry Rickards, had died the year before. His vast Tivoli empire was now managed by the owner of the Sydney Stadium, Hugh D. Macintosh, a man who wanted to build an empire of his own. The Tivoli circuit's major competitor was also undergoing changes. James Brennan's National Amphitheatre chain, the second vaudeville chain, had recently been taken over by Benjamin Fuller, the man who hired Carrie Moore.

Vaudeville had a reputation as the lesser art when compared to the legitimate theatre. This was particularly true in Melbourne, where such distinctions were an important part of life. Carrie's new career path was one which invited criticism from the media and from her former friends and associates with Williamson. This stigma combined with the scandal attached to her marital affairs lingered over Carrie in Australia.

Her continuing rift with J.C. Wiliamson also contributed to her lukewarm reception by the critics. Williamson had a monopoly on legitimate theatre in Australia, and Carrie was persona non grata on his stages. This left her with little choice but to appear in vaudeville and risk the disapproval of the Australian theatrical establishment.

Carrie opened in Melbourne on Monday 25 June. It was a rainy night, but the theatre was crowded. Carrie sang 'The Last Waltz' and 'A Woman's Eyes' and performed a telephone sketch called 'All Alone'. The crowds were enthusiastic and welcomed the local girl home with warm applause. Carrie's performance was given sparse attention by the mainstream press. *The Age* mentioned her appearance but made little comment on its quality. It was a typical reaction to a vaudeville act.

Carrie worked in Melbourne for a month. It was a short engagement, but there were more to come. Her next appearance was at the National Amphitheatre, known locally as 'The Nash', in Sydney.

The audience went wild when Carrie's name appeared on the boards, *The Referee* said,

> There was a roar from the crowded audience – a friendly sort of roar – when the name of the clever Australian was shown on the 'signboards' of the proscenium.

Carrie had left Australia, but she had not been forgotten by the Sydney public and they flocked to the Nash to see her for the first time in five years. What they saw was Carrie Moore as they had never seen her before. She entered the stage wearing a dainty, demure evening dress and the scene behind her was an equally demure drawing room. As applause echoed through the auditorium, Carrie gently acknowledged it with a courteous nod. She sang 'Dear Old Bow Bells' and the telephone song, 'I'm All Alone'. Then she performed a recitation of 'A Woman's Eyes' to piano accompaniment, which finished her short turn. However, it was not enough for the crowd who clamorously recalled her. In response to their shouts she performed an imitation of Gertie Millar, the star of George Edwardes's productions in England. Carrie had met Gertie and this familiarity lent veracity to her imitation. Carrie was an accomplished mimic and she was drawing on skills that she had learned with George Lauri and the Royal Comic Opera Company so many years before.

The newspaper reviews were complimentary, but short. *The Referee* said that she was 'completely successful' and added that

> During her stage career in Australia, Carrie Moore was lacking in refinement and repose. Her work was of the slap dash order, and her singing was at times wild and uncontrolled. Now she is a stylish artist and her voice is kept well 'in hand'.

Carrie attracted crowded houses throughout August and Ben Fuller publically declared that Carrie was worth far more than her wage of £100 a week. Later in the run, she changed her program by introducing some new songs, including 'Strolling', 'Put your arms around me honey' and 'Mimic May'.

There were some negative reviews and *Theatre Magazine* had some critical comments to make about Carrie's desertion of musical comedy. According to the magazine Carrie drew good crowds but her performance was disappointing. The writer sarcastically described her as 'eagerly' returning in response to 'sparingly given applause'. The criticism may have stemmed from an inherent prejudice against vaudeville or perhaps it was the lingering influence of J.C. Williamson. *Theatre Magazine* was a traditional publication that concentrated on legitimate theatre. In fact, the writer suggested that Carrie should stick to what she knew best, 'grace of movement and pretty light acting'. It was a patronising comment which did not consider the versatility of the actress. Carrie had performed in many musical comedies that had a strong variety element. Her vaudeville act capitalised on her skills as a comedienne and it gave her a respite from the long grind associated with a successful musical comedy career.

Carrie continued her vaudeville performances and travelled to the Brisbane Royal after the engagement in Sydney. She had family in Brisbane so the visit served a dual purpose. It was the last engagement under her contract with Fullers so she was then free to pursue her own interests.

Her Own Company

The Fullers contract gave Carrie financial security but the focus on her career had not helped her marriage. After fulfilling her obligations, Carrie, or more probably Percy, decided to form a touring company. Percy, now styling himself her manager, was billed at some stages of the tour as producer.

In November 1912, the Carrie Moore Comedietta company performed in Auckland, New Zealand. They moved on to Wellington for Christmas and spent the holiday season in the dominion. In New Zealand the company included Percy Clifton as the principal comedian and Mr Percy Dalton an eccentric dancer. Carrie sang 'That Last Waltz' and other popular tunes. The company received very positive reviews

Then they crossed the Tasman and travelled to Queensland, where they performed in country areas, including Rockhampton and Charters Towers in the north of the state.

Following that, they journeyed south to Brisbane. Whilst there, Carrie and Percy indulged their love of fast driving. They both enjoyed luxury vehicles and their speed. However, the Brisbane police did not share the couple's enthusiasm and they were taken into custody for exceeding the speed limit. They were only held for a short time because Carrie, in her best theatrical manner, threatened to sue for wrongful arrest. The matter was quietly dropped by the authorities.

From Queensland the company travelled by rail to Adelaide and then by boat to Western Australia. By 21 March 1913 they were in Perth.

The company opened at Her Majesty's Perth on 22 March. Their first production was *In the Soup*, a farce by Sydney Grundy. It was Carrie's first non singing role since her brief stint with Ernest Shand in *A Night Out* in 1897. It was also her first appearance in Western Australia since 1903.

Soon the company was on its way to Tasmania. They arrived in Hobart in late May and the company now included Carrie's friend, Maud Chetwynd. In Hobart, the company presented farces which included songs which were inappropriate for the productions. Nonetheless, the singing capitalised on Carrie's reputation and ensured that audiences attended shows which had recently played in the city.

In Hobart they gained a new producer/manager too. Carrie Moore was now being presented by that man of the world, Mr P.P. Bigwood, whose name appeared above hers in advertisements and billboards.

Pre-publicity for the season included an interview with Carrie by the Hobart *Mercury* newspaper. The reporter described her as

> an attractive, bright, winsome lady full of animation, appearing to interest herself in everything and unaffectedly displaying all the graces that may be expected to be observed in a queen of comic opera and musical comedy.

Carrie regaled the interviewer with details of her career in London and Australia with emphasis on her overseas success. She carefully mentioned her husband and ensured that his name appeared beside her own on the printed page. The couple was still sharing their hobby of motoring and planned to drive around the little island to see the sights. Their enthusiasm had survived the brief arrest in Brisbane.

The company played in Hobart for a month and then motored to Launceston. The small company touring experience was a new one for Carrie, who was accustomed to appearing in the largest theatres with huge casts in both Australia and London. Although she had left musical comedy for a less demanding schedule, the constant touring and the heavy responsibility of an eponymous company was far from an ideal situation.

Managing a company of actors, paying their salaries, organising publicity, transport and sorting out the various problems attendant on these responsibilities was both time consuming and expensive. The

Carrie Moore Company did not lighten her workload. In fact, as the only 'name' player, it added to her burden. Percy's role as manager was also a source of conflict. 'Good houses' were probably not adequate to meet his expectations, and the already shaky relationship began to collapse under the added stress.

1913 was noticeable for another event. J.C. Williamson had died in Paris that July surrounded by his wife and daughters. He had made his last appearance on an Australian stage the previous February when he performed at a benefit for Scott's lost Antarctic expedition. He and Carrie had never reconciled. It was the end of an era for Australian theatre and Carrie must have been upset that the man who created her career was gone.

She had forsaken musical comedy because of the demands it made on her time and the associated stress, but she had no choice but vaudeville in Australia. Despite Williamson's death, she was still considered unemployable by his company. Old grudges died hard in the theatrical world of the early twentieth century.

In October, Carrie played in vaudeville in Brisbane with the famous Ted Holland Company and later that month, she was back at work for Fullers in Sydney at the National Amphitheatre. The Carrie Moore Company had collapsed and the engagement with Fullers coincided with a public declaration that her marriage was over.

'A midsummer madness' was how she described her union to Percy in an interview with *Theatre Magazine*. She ascribed her lack of judgment to 'a sloppy heart'.

Vowing to dedicate herself to the stage, she denied rumours that she had pawned her famous diamond collection for her husband. 'All the diamonds and property I ever had are quite safe,' she informed the curious public..

The interview was Carrie's declaration of independence. However, although she separated from the man the magazine called 'her quondam husband', she never took the final step of divorce. Perhaps the dubious legality of the union made divorce unnecessary.

It had been a turbulent five years for Carrie. The high point of *The Merry Widow* had quickly been overwhelmed by a series of personal scandals which began with her involvement with Percy Bigwood. Shaken by these experiences, Carrie tried to find solace in her art. Her return to vaudeville in 1913 was an attempt to redirect her life and gain financial stability.

Although she declared that she 'still had her diamonds', it is likely that she had little left of the earnings from her stage career. Financial irresponsibility was a feature of Percy's character. His obligations to Ivy Salvin and Bessie Bigwood and their children may also have contributed to a lack of funds.

Fortunately by the end of 1913, Carrie was in demand once again. She was offered a role which was familiar and financially lucrative. It was Christmas, it was pantomime season and one of the world's best principal boys was available. Christmas 1913, the last Christmas before the outbreak of World War I was to prove a lucky one for Carrie Moore.

Aladdin

In December 1913, George Willoughby announced that he was producing Sydney's first Christmas pantomime for seven years, *Aladdin*. The workers at Willoughby's Adelphi Theatre had been working for months preparing the auditorium and the manager had hired Lester Brown, a New York producer, to ensure that the latest sensations from the northern hemisphere were included in the show.

He also added local appeal by hiring two of the most popular actresses in Australia, Carrie Moore and Grace Palotta. Carrie played the principal boy, Aladdin, whilst Grace was given the role of Koko, the captain of the guard. There was a rivalry between the two ladies and there was much interest in theatrical circles about what problems this would cause the production.

Carrie and Grace had known each other for many years. Before Carrie went to England in 1903, she had co-starred with Grace in Royal Comic Opera Company productions. In fact, the two ladies had first met in 1895 when Carrie, an ambitious teenager, had sung for Grace at her Uncle William's home. Since that time, Carrie had gained fame and notoriety in England, she knew she was a star and expected to be treated as such. Grace was also a diva and the gossips speculated that *Aladdin* would be a stormy and troubled show. Nonetheless, on Christmas Eve 1913, the pantomime opened to a huge crowd at the Adelphi Theatre in Haymarket, Sydney.

Carrie was a vivacious and gorgeously dressed Aladdin. She wore vivid colours and short tights which showed off 'the best pair of legs in the show'. She had matured and was more full figured than her early years, but her physical charms had not lessened. She was one of the few ladies who could play principal boy without using a cloak to cover her shortcomings.

Her refined principal boy was a hit with the first night audience and her song, 'The trail of the lonesome pine', was rewarded with a double encore. She was very comfortable in the role because of her vast experience in London pantomime. Her performance proved that she was a genuine expert in the part.

The pantomime was produced in the grand tradition of the Williamson shows of previous years. The sets were elaborate, the costumes lavish and the jokes topical and pointed. The show included specialty turns such as wrestling ponies, but the highlight was undoubtedly the wonderful ragtime revue. Lester Brown's influence was an important part of *Aladdin* and it was his American experience that led to the revue being included in the show. It closed the first act and involved a large group of beautiful girls dancing ragtime on top of a platform that stretched over the stalls and ran the entire length of the theatre. The effect of a double row of red lights, ragtime music and tightly clad showgirls was a hit with audiences and critics. Its popularity lead to a mini revival of ragtime in Sydney, and ragtime music was incorporated into shows at rival theatres to capitalise.

Whilst *Aladdin* championed the cause of ragtime, Hugh MacIntosh took the Tivoli in another direction. That Christmas saw the introduction of another novelty in Sydney, the tango. The dance was considered scandalous because of its close body contact and revealing dresses. Ladies wore long flowing gowns with long slits up the legs, whilst their partner held them close in the passionate dance. Although the true tango had been modified for Anglo audiences, it still ruffled feathers amongst the wowser element in Australia.

MacIntosh capitalised on the scandal by introducing a series of tango teas. The tango teas drew huge crowds and focused on displays of the dance. Whilst watching, the audience in the stalls and dress circle were served tea. The combination was novel entertainment and proved to be a significant competitor to the pantomime.

But *Aladdin* maintained its popularity and Carrie was in a hugely successful Christmas production in Australia's biggest city. Her singing and charisma were praised by critics and the show had high attendances. Towards the end of the run, a new aspect was added to the matinees and toys were given to all children who attended. Certainly that demographic was not being catered to by the tango teas.

Aladdin drew over 50,000 people to the Adelphi that Christmas season. It continued to attract good crowds through its nine-week stay. However, the company had other commitments and had to leave Sydney to tour New Zealand.

On 25 February 1914, over 160 members of the *Aladdin* company arrived in Wellington, New Zealand. The contingent included Carrie, Grace Palotta, Nellie Fallon and the famous wrestling ponies. It also included some new cast members, tango experts Fred Oswald and Margot Maurice. George Willoughby had learnt from the Sydney experience and planned to introduce tango teas to New Zealand. However, the pantomime came first and on 26 February Aladdin opened at the Opera House in Wellington to tremendous critical and popular acclaim.

The whole production was imbued with an air of joy and enthusiasm, and the audience was carried along by its sheer exuberance. In many ways the pantomime defied modern trends by having two ladies playing the principal boys, because contemporary fashion was to have the part played by men. Yet the traditional choice proved popular with New Zealand crowds and critics and the latter commented favourably on the physical charms of Grace Palotta and Carrie.

During the tour, Carrie kept a relatively low profile and Grace took centre stage giving interviews and hosting the tango teas.

An Adelaide minister had called the tango 'the latest heresy in dancing' and the whole of Wellington was subsequently anxious to witness the scandalous dance. The tango teas as held in New Zealand were blatantly based upon the successful model pioneered by Hugh MacIntosh in Sydney. For half a crown, people in the dress circle could witness demonstrations of the dance, a fashion parade and have afternoon tea. For one shilling, those in the stalls could watch the show without refreshments.

The first tango tea in New Zealand occurred on 2 March. Carrie did not participate in the dancing, being content to sing a song from the pantomime. However, like the other ladies, she wore a daring dress which had the skirts draped to slightly open at the front. This was particularly necessary for the dancers, who could trip on their skirts whilst doing the intricate steps of the tango. The skirts opened, but they concealed most of the ladies legs except the ankle. According to the New Zealand *Free Lance*, this was quite acceptable. The ladies capitalised by adorning their ankles with bracelets and the flamboyant Grace Palotta wore an anklet sparkling with brilliants.

The audiences at the tango teas were huge and all the standing areas were full. They were so popular that people sat on the stairs two deep, but many in the crowd were expecting to see a scandalous exhibition of a daring dance and went home disappointed. The form of tango imported to Australia and New Zealand was very mild and lacked the risqué element of the original. The revelation of ankles and an occasional knee did not live up to the anticipation of the young men of Wellington.

But the pantomime with its two leading ladies clad in tights may have filled the gap. *Aladdin* was immensely popular. Soon the company travelled from Wellington to Napier and further to Auckland. Grace Palotta continued to garner the most attention, although Carrie was recognised for her excellent portrayal of Aladdin.

At the end of March 1914 the company was in Auckland. The pantomime alternated with the tango teas and both were very successful. In Auckland the company devoted some time to raising money for charity. When they learned that the city was in need of an ambulance, a charity drive was organised. The principals of the cast were placed upon wagons and paraded around the city streets asking for money from passersby. Comedian, Percy Clifton, offered a kiss from Carrie for a quid. A young man was brave enough to make an offer and made his way to the platform where Carrie sat like an enthroned queen. He nervously approached her and she willingly kissed him on the lips. The company collected a substantial sum for the ambulance fund and also did a charity performance for the cause.

By the beginning of April, the New Zealand tour was over and it was time for the cast and crew to travel to Australia for an Easter season of the pantomime.

The Early War Years

The Carrie Moore who returned to her homeland was no longer a slim teenager. She was a mature woman of thirty-one, plumper in the body and fuller of face. Yet her trademark vivacity and charm still drew audiences wherever she appeared.

The *Aladdin* pantomime company returned to Australia and appeared at Hobart's Theatre Royal that May. The ragtime revue astounded Tasmanian audiences. After Hobart, the company, complete with wrestling ponies and tango teas, travelled to Adelaide and by June they had arrived in Melbourne for an extended stay.

Aladdin opened at the Princess Theatre on Wednesday 17 June 1914. With Grace Palotta and Carrie Moore sharing the stage, the pantomime was an enormous success and both ladies received rapturous welcomes from the audience. Critics described the talented actresses as being tastefully dressed and shapely in form, two necessary ingredients for a successful production.

But events in the wider world soon overshadowed the pantomime. On 29 June Archduke Franz Ferdinand was assassinated in Sarajevo, and on 5 August, at 1.30 p.m., the Australian newspapers printed special editions. England had declared war on Germany, which meant that Australia was also at war. The war to end all wars was enthusiastically embraced by the Australian population and young men raced to enlist fearing that they would miss the fun. Everybody thought it would end by Christmas.

The theatrical establishment was quick to embrace the enthusiasm. The managers knew that their role in wartime was to provide distraction and fan patriotism. Farces, comedies and nationalistic pantomimes were all features of World War One Australian theatre.

After *Aladdin* finished, Carrie travelled to New Zealand for a vaudeville season with Fullers. Whilst there, she helped raise money for the Belgian Relief Fund. With other performers, Carrie sold flowers and kisses and raised £90 for the fund. Percy Bigwood was also in New Zealand, and Carrie probably saw him. He had joined the army and when he enlisted gave her as his next of kin. Although separated, the husband and wife were in contact and Carrie, who had experienced war before, now had a personal interest in its progress.

In January 1915 Carrie returned to the Australian vaudeville circuit, doing a short season at the National Amphitheatre in Sydney. She proved a popular addition to the bill and drew good crowds every night. It was an unusual New Year for Carrie, one of the few in which she did not perform in pantomime.

She travelled to Melbourne in March and appeared at the Bijou Theatre. Her turn consisted of impersonating a Yorkshire girl and singing several songs in character. She charmed the theatre with her version of 'That's Not the Way in Yorkshire'. During every performance she selected a young child from the audience to sing a chorus and at the end of the run she gave a prize to the most talented youngster.

Bad news came in April. On 23 April, Lance Corporal Percy Bigwood of the Auckland Infantry Battalion died of pneumonia. It was a shock for Carrie, who despite the problems in her marriage had maintained contact with her estranged husband. Fortunately, she was living with her mother at the time of his death, and this provided some comfort.

Work was another comfort. By June she was rehearsing in Sydney with the Bert La Blanc revue company. The company was under contract to Fullers and included producer Lester Brown. It was this dual connection which ensured Carrie's addition to the show.

Revues were a popular format in vaudeville theatres during the war, and combined music, dancing, sketches and satirical songs. The defection of quality vaudeville artists to the front left vacancies in the talent pool. Revues filled half a vaudeville program and were cheaper than high-class vaudeville acts.

Carrie stayed with the Bert La Blanc company until late 1915. The company interspersed revues with charity performances and became very popular with audiences and fellow theatricals. However, by November, she had left the company and was hired to perform in the Adelphi Theatre's Christmas pantomime, *Dick Whittington*.

The Adelphi Theatre in Sydney had been remodelled by New Zealand architect Henry White, who had redesigned it to bring the audience closer to the stage. This created a cosy atmosphere for Carrie and the cast when they opened in late December 1915.

It was a typical pantomime for the era. Fantasy, topical references, exotic locations and several specialty turns all served to distract the audience from what was becoming a long war. Typically for the time the pantomime also encouraged patriotic fervour with rousing anthems. In this case the song was 'We'll get Right There Bye and Bye', sung by Miss Kathleen Mack dressed in a captain's uniform.

Carrie again proved her expertise as a principal boy and she was popular with audiences and praised by critics. The latter were quick to note that she was plumper and more rounded than in previous years. Carrie had a popular hit with the song 'What's the Good of Moonlight', a sentimental ballad about the trials of love.

The fantasy of pantomime was sometimes interrupted with the poignancy of reality. Fifty wounded soldiers attended one performance, and one had lost both his legs. The cast, moved by their presence, took up a collection and showered the men with tobacco and cigarettes. At this, the audience spontaneously erupted into a chorus of 'Rule Britannia'. Thus did the cruelty of war and the fantasy of theatre co-exist in Sydney in late 1915.

It was a hugely popular production. Full houses greeted every show and it continued into February, when it was shipped to Brisbane for a brief season. After two weeks there, the pantomime opened at the Princess Theatre in Melbourne

It opened on Saturday 8 April 1916 at one of Carrie's favourite theatres. The audience was large and the show full of the usual references to war and topical themes such as the Census Office and the Panama exhibition. In an unusual twist and as an obvious reference to the times, the fairy godmother was encased in armour. As principal boy, Carrie was praised for her lack of sentimentality, and her ability to minimise this element was a feature of her performance.

When she reached Melbourne, Carrie's voice was suffering from strain and stress. This was noticed by critics who suggested she was breathing wrongly during the songs. However, it was obvious that Carrie had a more severe problem. Carrie's voice did not improve a month after opening and it was soon announced that she would be taking time off to undergo an operation for throat trouble. Her voice was her livelihood and she had to be careful. She took a prolonged period of time off to recover from the throat operation. It was the first substantial break that she had experienced since she was thirteen years old. However, Carrie loved theatrical life and it took more than a sore throat to keep her from the footlights.

During this time she was in contact with J.C. Williamson Limited. Although the Guv'nor J.C. Williamson, had passed away, the company still used his name and held some of his prejudices. It had been nine years since Carrie had appeared in a Williamson production and perhaps the company managers thought it was time to forgive and forget. Carrie was still a draw in Melbourne and Sydney and she was an accomplished, versatile performer. In July 1917, she announced to Australian Variety that she would be reappearing in a J.C. Williamson production later that year.

Firstly, she performed for Fullers; it was an opportunity to test her healed throat in a less demanding role than musical comedy. The vehicle was a farce called *A Little Bit of Fluff* and it opened in July at the Grand Opera House in Sydney.

The reappearance of Carrie Moore on a Sydney stage enticed a large number of Sydneysiders to the theatre. However, she was almost unrecognisable as 'the bit of fluff'. The *Bulletin* said that she looked 'like an elder sister of herself down from the country'. In order to identify herself, Carrie entered the stage humming a few bars from *Florodora* and this elicited warm applause of recognition from the spectators. She was plumper than she had been for years – obviously the forced absence from the stage had caused her to gain weight – but her voice was still tuneful. She was allotted the only singing parts in the farce and one prescient song was entitled 'Wait until we get married'.

At the conclusion of the first performance, Carrie received many bouquets and a black kitten in a box for good luck. The cat must have worked because the farce was a popular and critical hit in Sydney and played for a month.

In September, Carrie began rehearsals for her long-awaited return to the Williamson stage in the comedy *Mr Manhattan*. The play included several song and dance numbers and also featured reputable Williamson stars such as Arthur Stigant, a reliable comedian, and Maggie Dickinson, a premier dancer. Carrie, described as 'plump and matronly', took the second lead. The show opened in Melbourne in late September, and received terrible notices. The public were kinder and *Mr Manhattan* remained at Her Majesty's until the end of October, when the cast headed to Sydney.

It was better received there by both critics and public. *Mr Manhattan* employed some broad humour and perhaps the warmer reception in Sydney was due to that city's more liberal social attitudes. Carrie was praised for her acting and her singing and *The Referee* said that she was 'strikingly like the Carrie of the good old days of yore'.

Although the critics admitted that she did not have the best voice in the show, they admired her ability to convey the sentiment of a song saying that 'she is an artist in her kind and in point of all round artistry her songs are the best thing in the show'.

This was to be one of Carrie's last performances in Sydney for many years. The song 'Wait until we're married' had been a signal pointing to her next project. Carrie Moore had found her next husband.

Remarriage and the Later War Years

1918 marked the final year of the Great War and as Australians prepared for Empire Day that May, the soldiers on the front suffered appalling conditions. In Europe, a long heatwave had been broken by thunderstorms that tuned the trenches into muddy slimy pits. Gas shells exploded during the night, whilst the sound of aeroplanes mingled with artillery and rain during the day, resulting in an eerie cacophony. The war was a dirty revolting mess of death and mud, but the allies were slowly winning the long battle of attrition.

In Sydney, the Empire Day celebrations featured many patriotic sentiments. There was a military concert at the Town Hall and the late Queen Victoria's statue was festooned with flags and bunting.

In the midst of the celebrations and memorials Carrie Moore prepared for another personal milestone. Despite her experiences with Percy, Carrie was getting married for a second time. She later said that she had fallen in love with two men in her life and married both of them. Her unfortunate affair with Tyson was conveniently forgotten.

The lucky second husband was Horace Vernon Bartlett, also known as John or Jack Wyatt. He was a Victorian who was born in Ballarat in 1878. In 1902 he married a lady called Maudie Moore, and the pair remained married until 1918. In February that year, Maudie sued Horace for divorce and gave desertion as the reason. Horace seems to have been a ladies' man, and it is probable that the impetus for the divorce came from his involvement with Carrie, who was eager to avoid the scandal of her first marriage.

Wyatt, as he was more familiarly known, was an importer and bookmaker. More importantly he was a man of wealth who made up to £7,000 a year. Jack insisted that Carrie give up the stage to marry him and she agreed. It seemed that the rebellious Sandow Girl was finally following the traditional path.

Carrie was living alone in a house in Sydney before the wedding. Like many theatrical people, she was superstitious and she believed in the spirit world. One night as she was in bed, she received a ghostly visitation, Percy Bigwood appeared and he seemed concerned.

> I even recognised his old tweed suit with the leather buttons. I had a little chat with him and put his fears at rest, then he dematerialised.

After all the stress and strain she had endured with him, she still thought of her first husband fondly.

Her second wedding took place at a private home with a minister performing the ceremony. Carrie, whose religious leanings had become more pronounced as she aged, insisted upon a spiritual aspect to the service. None of her family acted as witnesses and she listed her father's occupation as being a man of independent means. The humble origins of the Moore family in Geelong were conveniently forgotten by its most famous member.

Carrie's marriage maintained her upper-class lifestyle and John Wyatt was very generous. He provided her with an annual clothing allowance of £500 and each year he gave her £100 to spend at the Melbourne Cup horse race. The couple maintained two houses in Sydney, a home at Coogee, a beachside suburb to the east of Sydney, and a flat in the exclusive Macquarie Street.

The 1920s were the era of the flapper, the Charleston and the jazz age. Moving pictures were accessible to the common man and posing a threat to the theatre as entertainment. Women were more daring, smoking and dancing and sometimes earning their own living, much to the disgust of conservative society. The end of the war released people from fear and a tidal wave of new music, new technology and new social attitudes swept the world.

It was an era that would have suited Carrie Moore the Sandow Girl, but that girl had retired and lived a quiet married life circulating with family and friends.

Carrie spent some time during the 1920s visiting family and when she went to Geelong she travelled in style. She still loved fast cars, and her husband, knowing this, imported Australia's first Rolls Royce for her use. Carrie used the vehicle frequently. When she visited Geelong in the Rolls, children from the neighbouring streets would gather to watch it rumble down the street. The grand diva would alight from this magnificent car, thrilling adults and children alike with her fine clothes and sparkling gems. During her marriage, the famous diamond collection increased, and she was remembered as having diamonds on each of her fingers. Evidently the spirit of the 'little exhibitionist' was still strong.

Carrie was the Moore family's acknowledged star. Although her sisters also had theatrical careers, it was Carrie who was considered the greatest and most famous member of the clan. Her visits to Geelong were grand occasions, and whilst there she stayed with an old childhood friend, Mrs Glover, on Toorak Parade. In contrast, her sisters would stay in the more modest home of their brother, but Carrie always had to live in the finest surroundings.

During the decade, Carrie was rarely mentioned by the press, but her name was featured every time a revival of *The Merry Widow* was produced. Sonia was her signature role and she was forever remembered as Australia's first Merry Widow. Nobody could take that legend from her.

She had many strong friendships in the international theatrical world; amongst them were Ivy Scott and Billie Burke. Her friendship with Ivy dated back to their childhood days, and it was a testament to Carrie's loyalty that she remained true to her early friends. Later she would visit both ladies frequently.

Carrie seems to have been happy as the grand dame of the Australian theatre, her reputation as a married woman was spotless, and her status as a retired actress very high. She had diamonds and the leisure to spend time with her family and friends which was a luxury that she had not previously enjoyed. Wyatt was a generous man and money was not a problem. For most of the 1920s Carrie lived a private life as Mrs John Wyatt, but it was not to last. Wyatt, like Percy before him, was a philanderer and by the end of the decade, Carrie was filing for divorce.

Legend

The Wall Street crash of 1929 had destroyed the optimism and exuberance of the flapper era. Times were hard, unemployment high and some unfortunate people in Sydney lived in ghetto encampments like Happy Valley in La Perouse.

Carrie Moore and Jack Wyatt were not badly affected by the crash and had lived together on a lavish scale until 1931. In that year she discovered that he was conducting an illicit affair with a woman called Kathleen Bayers. Devastated by his betrayal and haunted by memories of her first marriage, Carrie fled overseas to visit her sisters.

When Carrie returned to Australia in March 1932, it was to terrible news. Her mother, Mary, who had always supported her daughter's career, had died whilst she was overseas. Mary had passed away peacefully at the home of her son Cliff in Geelong; she was seventy-seven years old.

In December that year, Carrie applied for alimony from Wyatt. It was an admission that the marriage was over and was a difficult step for the religious Carrie to take. The press coverage of the case added to her distress, as it detailed every aspect of the marriage and Wyatt's adultery.

Carrie applied for £25 week alimony from her husband, who was described as an importer. Wyatt opposed the application, stating that his income was much less than his wife stated. Finally the magistrate awarded the actress a rate of £12 a week, a very small sum for the profligate Carrie.

In March 1933, she took a more formal step towards dissolving the union; she applied for and received a judicial separation from her husband.

1933 was a big year for her. It was the year that turned the Merry

Widow into a bona fide legend of the Australian stage. The occasion that created a legend was the closure of Her Majesty's Theatre in Sydney.

Taxation, the movies and economic depression had combined to make one of Sydney's grand old theatres unprofitable and impractical. The stage that had hosted George Rignold, Nellie Melba, Pavlova and Genee, and countless performances by the Royal Comic Opera Company, was being demolished. Its final night was 10 June 1933.

The last performance was fittingly *Maid of the Mountains*, starring Gladys Moncrieff, Australia's premier singing star. Gladys was the leading diva of the Williamson stable and occupied the position that once was Carrie Moores. One of her favourite roles was Sonia, in *The Merry Widow*.

The theatre was decorated with flags and hosted a full house that final night. The crowd was an impressive one in the midst of depression.

Carrie was one of many guests of honour and participated in a special feature of the show. After the final song of *Maid of the Mountains* faded and the last act had finished, the famous brown velvet curtain rose again to reveal a parade of historic performers who had graced the stage. The people represented included George Rignold, Sarah Bernhardt, Howard Vernon, Florence Young, Nellie Melba, Pavlova and finally, as herself, dressed as the Merry Widow, Miss Carrie Moore. Her appearance caused wild and loud applause from the large audience. It was recognition of her status as a legend, forever engraved in Australian theatrical history as the first Merry Widow.

After speeches and a round of songs, including an emotional rendition of 'Auld Lang Syne', the audience sadly filed out the doors the last time. However, a special after-hours celebration was held on stage for the actors and special guests.

The firm JCW invited everybody from stage hands to ticket sellers, to a party which included supper and dancing and of course fond reminisces. Carrie was amongst the party guests, who danced to 3 a.m. on the old stage.

Her appearance that night cemented her position as a legend of the Australian theatre. It also fixed her as the Merry Widow in the collective memories of a generation of playgoers. Carrie and Sonia would forever be entwined. The night gave her an opportunity to renew connections with the current management of Williamsons. The connection was to prove fruitful some months later.

In August 1933 Carrie appeared in the musical *Music in the Air*. It was a J.C. Williamson production at the Theatre Royal in Sydney. The show starred English actor Sylvia Welling, who was supported by a cast including Sydney Wheeler and Cecil Kellaway. Carrie had a small role as Frau Direktor Kirschner. In a strange twist, Ivy Scott, her former partner in *Djin Djin*, was playing the role in New York at the time.

The musical, unlike Carrie's earlier work, had a moral theme, and was not the confection of previous years. This was an indication of the changing tastes of the Depression era. In the midst of this era, Carrie was lucky to find work, and *Music in the Air* was her last major appearance on an Australian stage.

Although it was not her last offer. Williamsons was so impressed with Carrie's work in the show that they offered her a revival of *The Merry Widow*. However, Carrie was a realist and knew that she could not measure up to the girl she was at twenty-six. She laughed at the offer saying,

> The idea flatters and thrills me but I have a picture of myself as Sonia when I was 26. I have a mirror and I have ears. No I will not play The Merry Widow.

Carrie took her position as an Australian theatrical legend very seriously and remained interested in every aspect of theatre, although her appearances were rare. Carrie was uniquely generous and was willing to sing at every type of performance, including benefits, charity and amateur shows. Of course, she was always interested in any production of *The Merry Widow*.

She lived in Sydney, but often visited relatives in Geelong; obviously the town held a special place in her heart. In 1936 she sang several songs at a benefit concert for violinist Basil Jones. That same year she sang for a Geelong woman, Elizabeth Andrews, who was celebrating her 104th birthday. Carrie sang 'Twilight', to the delight of Mrs Andrews and her guests.

Carrie was restless and loved to travel; she considered it a great educator. She also had family and friends scattered around the world and spent many years visiting them. In 1936 she left Australia for an extensive three-year trip to the United States and England. The allowance from her husband was small and it did not cover her expenses. Carrie always liked to live extravagantly and she began to use her diamonds to finance her frequent overseas jaunts.

In England she spent time with her sister Olive, who had married British actor Harry Barrett. Olive and Harry lived in Shepherds Bush and their home was a popular meeting place for theatrical people. Carrie enjoyed the atmosphere of gossip and nostalgia at the house.

She was in England in September 1938 when British Prime Minister Neville Chamberlain met Hitler at Munich and seemed to have averted a terrible war. Chamberlain was hailed as a hero in England, and in Australia, the Prime Minister, Mr Lyons, proposed a national day of thanksgiving. Lyons said that the agreement promised a lasting peace.

On 9 November that year, Carrie Moore made her final appearance on a London stage. The theatre was the Coliseum and the occasion was the annual Royal Variety Performance. Carrie was asked by producer Lupino Lane to join the show. She had known Lane since her pantomime days in England. Carrie joined a group which included Irene Vanbrugh, Mabel Love and Seymour Hicks for a performance of the latest sensation, 'The Lambeth Walk', which was the grand finale of the show. Her inclusion with these elite performers was an indication of her status as a performer in England. Carrie later told Australian reporters about the experience.

> We rehearsed at the Coliseum for three hours one day. It was a real reunion of former stars. You can imagine how I felt after 20 years off the English stage.

That same night, in Germany, racist gangs attacked Jewish businesses, homes and synagogues in a night later christened Kristallnacht.

The next year, as war in Europe came closer, Carrie crossed the Atlantic to America and visited old friend Billie Burke. During Carrie's stay, Billie's daughter, Patricia, married dance instructor William Robert Stephenson in Beverley Hills California. It was a large society wedding and 200 people, many from Hollywood, attended. Carrie was a guest too, and described Patricia as 'a lovely girl'. Whilst in California, Carrie met several movie producers, and was offered some film roles. Unfortunately she was unable to accept due to visa restrictions. According to Carrie,

> Selznick pictures offered me the part of the English society woman in *Rebecca*, but I had to decline the offer.

Soon she was on her way back to Australia after a three-year absence. On the way home, she sang a solo for the ship's Christmas service. Carrie was greeted by reporters when she arrived in Sydney and gave them some memorable quotations, including the ever popular 'It is simply wonderful to be back in Sydney again'.

On Monday 4 September 1939, Australians woke up to newspaper headlines declaring that the country had joined Great Britain in declaring war on Germany. The theatre was quick to take up its traditional role as booster of morale and fund raiser.

It was Carrie's third war as a performer and she donated her time generously. She spent the war years travelling through Australia and appearing for various benefits and charities. She also broadened her repertoire and began to appear in the new media of radio, TV and films. She was one of few actresses who could adapt to new technology and thus became one of the rare performers who had appeared successfully in vaudeville, musical comedy, pantomime, radio, TV and movies.

In 1941, Carrie appeared at the old Players and Playgoers birthday and annual fete. It was held in Fitzroy Gardens in Melbourne and Carrie was a special guest. The association presented tableaux of famous performers but noticeably there was no representation of the Merry Widow. Carrie contributed to the event by singing several songs and telling old stories. Many tall tales were told that night. Her association with the Playgoers was typical of Carrie's continuing interest in Australian theatre and her willingness to appear at any event that promoted it.

Carrie spent most of the war years living in Sydney near her sister Lily. The two spent a great deal of time together. In 1942 Carrie began a radio career with Sydney station 2CH. She was involved with several radio broadcasts for the station.

The end of the war in 1945 meant that Carrie could safely travel again, and she almost immediately arranged to leave Australia. She took a short trip to the United States in 1945 and was offered several roles in movies, but they were not good enough.

> I did not like any of the parts offered to me and I have never yet played a part that did not really appeal to me.

In America she spent most of her time in Hollywood and stayed in the home of long time friend Ivy Scott. Ivy had a successful career on the American stage and was appearing in a production of *Song of Norway*.

Carrie spent Christmas of 1945 with Cecil Kellaway and his family. Kellaway had become a popular film actor and had appeared in five films that year. It was an indication of how close knit the theatrical scene was in Australia that Carrie could rely on these old friends for accommodation and company when overseas. She also spent some time with Billie Burke who Carrie described as 'my oldest and best friend in America'. She added that 'she has not changed at all since I last saw her six years ago'.

Urgent family business called Carrie back to Australia, but her stay was short. The next year she was overseas again visiting America, England and Africa.

> I visited England because I love it, America because I was invited by my sister and Africa simply because I had not been there before.

In New York she made her first appearance on television in a drama called *The Haunted Robe*. Carrie appreciated the unique abilities required for television acting and had three days to learn forty-two sides of manuscript. Fortunately, her memory was still good. Carrie insisted that television was for real actors with good memories and experience and she foresaw a bright future for former stage stars on the small screen.

Carrie was somewhat anxious about the make-up that was applied for the role, and remarked to the makeup artist, 'I hope you are not putting any more wrinkles into my face, dear?'

The busy girl replied to Carrie's relief, 'I'm not putting them in, dear, I'm taking them out.'

In 1949, her first film was released. She had a minor role in an Australian movie called *Sons of Matthew*. Carrie played a midwife and appeared at several premieres of the show.

She returned to Australia, arriving in Melbourne in 1950 and was met off the boat by her sister, Lily, her niece Mrs Hallett, the young Hallett boys, eleven-year-old twins Robby and Cliffy, and the Melbourne press. Carrie was particularly proud that the boys were singing with St Paul's choir.

> I'm looking forward to hearing them sing, It's nice to hear the Moore voice is being carried on.

Carrie had another story for the press too and she announced that she was writing an autobiography. Then she travelled to Sydney, and was met by the newspaper boys there. She was careful to give details of her sisters' doings and in particular she mentioned Lily's appearance at the Kings Theatre in Melbourne. Carrie also gave more details about the proposed autobiography. She told reporters that

> The Merry Widow will always be my favourite role because it combines everything – singing acting, dancing – and they have to be done properly.

It was another opportunity to promote her legend. Finally she added a wistful coda to the interview, 'I can't say whether I will do any more acting.'

The Final Curtain

It was 10.30 a.m. on a beautiful Sunday morning in Sydney. The sun sparkled on the harbour and light reflected off the windows of a private hotel in Elizabeth Bay on the eastern shore. The sounds of splashing bath water mingled with a tuneful soprano voice, floated through the thin walls and a male guest lifted his head from the newspaper he was reading.

'Good lord, that reminds me of Carrie Moore in *The Merry Widow* umpteen years ago.'

Another guest confirmed it. 'That is Carrie Moore. She's still singing the Merry Widow. She sings it every day in her bath.'

The first man was shocked. 'I thought she was dead.'

It was 1951 and Australia had changed greatly from the society it was in the roaring 1890s. Cinema and radio dominated popular entertainment and Australian theatre was undergoing a resurgence spurred by a new generation of post-war playwrights and a new vision of Australian culture brought on by the experience of World War II. The country was on the verge of immense change, the insular Anglo enclave was becoming a vibrant multicultural society.

Carrie Moore had changed too, but mostly physically. She was sixty-eight, a plump white-haired lady, living with her photos, mementoes and props of past glory. She still kept the dress she wore as Sonia in *The Merry Widow*. Emotionally and psychologically, Carrie still lived in the old world. She found many aspects of modern life distasteful. She was shocked by contemporary speech saying that it was 'riddled with vulgarity'.

Carrie was also concerned with respectability. Perhaps still influenced by the Edwardian notion that actresses were not respectable, she told a reporter that year how proud she was that scandal had never touched her name.

> I was just as unattainable to the rich men who paid fancy prices to see me from the boxes as I was to the poor men who paid sixpence to see me from the gallery.

In the 1950s the Bigwood affair was not scandalous, and the name Tyson was almost forgotten. Carrie was aware that she had a legendary role in Australian theatre and her press interviews were designed to reinforce her prestige and elevate her character. Her ability to tell a good story had not faded with age and in many ways she was still the young Carrie of the Edwardian era. She called everybody 'ladies' and 'gentlemen' and she spent a great deal of time reminiscing about her past triumphs, especially her role as Sonia in *The Merry Widow*.

Occasionally she would stand at a window of her small bedsit looking at the harbour, dredge up the words to 'I Don't Want to Play in Your Yard' and entertain the other guests with a rendition of the old tune. In many ways it was a sad and lonely life, but Carrie was comforted by religion and by a determined optimism. She knew that she had experienced a unique life and told a reporter that year that 'I see this life merely as a preliminary canter.' She often told friends, 'Every night of my life I thanked God for my talents.'

She was not entirely alone; her sister, Lily, an active stage actress, lived nearby and she was always welcomed home by her Geelong relatives. When visiting she maintained the style of a great lady and her niece Olive described her as 'always the grande dame, always beautifully dressed. She was an act all the time.'

Carrie had long realised that her legacy would be Sonia in *The Merry Widow* and she actively promoted it. This legacy was legitimised by the Australian press well into the 1950s. Her longevity in the memory of the Australian theatrical establishment was a testament to her intelligence and lasting talent.

In November 1952, a film version of *The Merry Widow* starring Lana Turner was released in Australia. The appearance of the film released a new wave of publicity for Carrie Moore, Australia's first Merry Widow. Carrie was invited to the premiere of the film in Melbourne and was asked for her opinion by the press corps. She was delighted to give it.

> It's a perfectly magnificent production, perfectly cast and headed by a charming and talented Lana Turner. I lived through every minute with her.

Described by the press as 'the original Merry Widow', seventy-year-old Carrie 'bubbled with laughter and fun' as she talked to the reporters.

While in Melbourne she attended Frankston's centenary celebrations as a special guest. She opened the Pioneers Exhibition and sang at variety concerts on two successive nights. She sang 'The Merry Widow' and *The Frankston Post* said that she had 'undiminished charm and almost as much pep at 70 as when she created the role of the Merry Widow'.

That November, she became a widow in reality when John Wyatt died. Wyatt left an estate of £27,000, most of which went to his brother, whilst the rest was bequeathed to the woman who shared his later life, Kathleen Beyer. Strangely, Kathleen, the woman who had replaced Carrie in Wyatt's life and the cause of their separation, lived quite close to Carrie in Sydney's Double Bay.

A year later, Carrie sued in court for increased maintenance from the estate. She was in a poor situation financially and had not worked for several years. At the time she was receiving £500 a year in maintenance, but it was not enough to cover her living expenses. She had been forced to leave her Macquarie Street, Sydney, flat because of the high rent. She informed the court through her solicitor that she was living in reduced circumstances in a bedsitting room in Elizabeth Bay for which she paid £4 a week. Carrie was also in debt to the taxation office, owing them a substantial sum. Given Carrie's life, it was unlikely that she had much experience with budgeting or bills.

Carrie won the case and was awarded a weekly income of £15 a week plus a lump sum of £500. £1,400 was set aside for taxation purposes. She was almost penniless at this stage and her only assets were listed as her personal clothing. It was obvious that most, if not all, of the famous diamond collection had been sold and the proceeds spent on travel and living expenses. The amount she was awarded from the court, combined with money she received from family and friends, was enough for her to go overseas again the next year.

She spent the years between 1954 and 1956 in London and New York visiting friends and relatives, seeing plays and keeping up with the latest in television and movies. She also sang at a benefit concert for disabled soldiers in London.

Carrie returned to Australia in April 1956. Singing was as natural as breathing to her, and on the boat trip home she displayed her talents. The grey-haired plump lady with the big voice entertained the passengers on the *Iberia* with old vaudeville songs and routines. She was still charming and vivacious and had the presence and attitude of a star. 'Why should I stop singing?' she would say. 'What did God give me a voice for?'

On her return, she stayed with her sister Lily in Sydney. She planned to finish her autobiography and eventually move back to Geelong.

Carrie stayed with Lily until September. She lived quietly but was not very well. In early September she suffered a heart attack and was bed ridden for the next few days. On 5 September at 5 a.m., she called out to Lily from her bedroom and asked her younger sister to hold her hand. Ten minutes later, still holding Lily's hand, she peacefully passed away.

Her death was front-page news, and there were many tributes.

> The death of Carrie Moore, severed one of the last links with Australia's most colorful theatrical epochs. Even at 74, Miss Moore retained until a few days before her death the vitality which made her the toast of the hansom cab and feather boa era.

One paper carried the headline 'She was our first Merry Widow.' The London *Times* also published a short obituary. Harry Bowden, the Sydney J.C. Williamson representative, paid tribute to Carrie.

She was one of the best troupers Australia produced and one of the most brilliant child artists.

Two themes emerged from the notices: that Carrie was Australian, and her association with *The Merry Widow*. Perhaps the most poignant tribute came from a self-confessed admirer, John Patrick Macguire, who published a memorial note in the *Sydney Morning Herald* at his own expense.

> Husky, Dusky Vivid True
> Steel true and blade straight.

On 7 September 1956 a short service was held in the chapel of Kinselas funeral home in Sydney. It was sparsely attended, much to the surprise of Carrie's niece, Olive.

> You would expect Carrie Moore in those days, to have lines of, you know, celebrities and everything there – I think brother and I were about the only two at the funeral parlour.

Afterwards, the small group proceeded to Eastern Suburbs Crematorium, where Carrie was cremated. The simple funeral was a stark contrast to the glamour and high-class lifestyle that Carrie had, but it was an accurate reflection of her last years.

The lady who had once earned £200 a week left an estate of only £500. Carrie had died almost penniless, but not alone. After the romances, the travel, the diva tantrums, the scandals, the successes and the failures, Carrie returned to the one aspect of her life that had never failed, her family.

Notes

Cover photo (courtesy of Neil Litchfield)
Carrie Moore and Andrew Higginson in *The Merry Widow*, postcard c. 1908

Early Years
Carrie Moore birth certificate
The Australasian, 9/6/1900

Djin Djin and Matsa
Town and Country Journal 20/5/1908
Dames, principal boys – and all that: a history of pantomime in Australia, by Viola Tait, South Melbourne: Macmillan, 2001
Djin Djin, programme March 1896
The Referee 1/4/1896
Matsa, Queen of Fire by Bert Royle and J.C. Williamson, programme 26 December 1896
Sydney Morning Herald (SMH) 1/3/1897

From Child Star to Diva
The Referee 7/7/1897
The Australasian 9/6/1900
Town and Country Journal 20/5/1908
SMH, 2/8/1897, 2/10/1897, 22/12/1897
The Age 1/11/1897, 7/3/1898
The Melbourne Herald 6/11/1957
Adelaide Advertiser 23/5/1898, 27/5/1898

The Royal Comic Opera Company
Sydney Mail 2/12/1899, 9/12/1899, 16/12/1899, 23/12/1899, 30/12/1899, 9/6/1900, 15/6/1900
SMH, 27/12/1899
The Age 26/2/1900
The Argus 26/2/1900
The Australasian 9/6/1900

Florodora and the Tyson Affair
The Age 24/10/00, 24/11/00, 15/12/00
The Referee 10/4/01
SMH 15/6/01
Punch 4/7/01, 22/8/01, 0/10/01
Daily Telegraph 5/12/01

Sharing the Stage
The Referee 7/5/02, 3/6/02
The Argus 21/7/02, 13/10/02

Carrie Departs
Sydney Mail 14/1/03, 4/2/03
Sunday Times 31/5/03
Programme, farewell performance of the Royal Comic Opera Company, 29/5/03.

Musical Comedy in England
Carriages at eleven: The story of the Edwardian Theatre by W Macqueen Pope. Hutchinson and Co. St Albans, 1947
Victorian and Edwardian Musical Shows http://www.halhkmusic.com/castlists/cingalee.html
The Times 7/3/ 1904, 23/2/1910
Postcard of Carrie Moore in the Cingalee c. 1904
Melbourne Herald 6 /11/1957
The Theatre Magazine, No. II Vol. I, London 1906 p. 54

Photo Bits London 14 /11/1906, pp. 28–29
– quoted on Footlight Notes http://members.tripod.com/ FootlightNotes/index.html
People Magazine 10/10/1951

The Merry Widow and the Bigwood Scandal
The Age 16/5/1908
The Sunday Times 27/9/1908
The Sydney Sportsman 30/9/1908
The Australasian 3/10/1908
SMH 5/10/1908, 6/10/1908
People Magazine 10/10/1951

Return to England
It's Behind You http:// www.its-behind-you.com/shakespeareliv.html
The Referee 10/2/1909, 7/8/1912
The Times April 1909
The Australasian 3/7/1909
The Otago Witness 4 /8/1909
The Times 23/2/1910, 18/9/1911, 19/4/1912
Evening Post 1/6/1912

Australasian Vaudeville Star
Evening Post April 1912, 3/5/1912
The Age 13/6/1912
The Referee 10/7/1912, August 1912
The Theatre September 1912 p. 15

Her Own Company
Evening Post 21/9/1912
The West Australian 21/3/1913
The Mercury 16 /6/1913
The Theatre Magazine 1/11/1913

Aladdin
The Referee 17/12/1913
SMH 26 /12/1913
Evening Post 25/2/1914, 27/2/1914, 14/11/1914

The Early War years
The Mercury 5/5/1914

Evening Post 27/4/1915
Australian Variety 7/7/1915
The Argus 15/3/1915
Australian Variety 29/12/1915, 3/5/1916, 11/7/1917, 8/8/1917

Remarriage and the Later War Years
Gwlad McLachlan, *Sentimental Journey, Geelong West Remembered*, radio programme 3/2/1994
Victorian marriage certificate, Caroline Ellen Moore and Horace Vernon Bartlett
People Magazine op. cit.

Legend
The Sun 16/12/1932
The Daily Telegraph 14/6/1933
Souvenir of Her Majesty's Theatre 1887–1933
J.C. Williamson magazine programme *Music in the Air* 19/8/1933
McLachlan op. cit.
The Times 10/11/1938
SMH 27/12/1939, 10/5/1946, 6/10/1950
Programme, The Old Players and Playgoers Birthday and Annual Fete, 6/12/1941
The Age Biography File, State Library of Victoria biography files. Various Clippings

The Final Curtain
People Magazine 10/10/1951
SMH 21/11/1953, 28/11/1953, 5/9/1956, 6/9/1956
McLachlan op. cit.
The Times 6/9/1956
Victorian death certificate, Caroline Ellen Wyatt 5/9/1956